POEMS 1967-1990

ESSENTIAL POETS SERIES

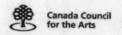

Canada Council   Conseil des Arts
for the Arts   du Canada

ONTARIO ARTS COUNCIL
CONSEIL DES ARTS DE L'ONTARIO

Guernica Editions Inc. acknowledges the support of
The Canada Council for the Arts.
Guernica Editions Inc. acknowledges the support of
the Ontario Arts Council.

LEN GASPARINI

THE BROKEN WORLD

POEMS 1967-1998

GUERNICA
TORONTO · BUFFALO · CHICAGO · LANCASTER (U.K.)
2005

Antonio D'Alfonso, editor
Guernica Editions Inc.
P.O. Box 117, Station P, Toronto (ON), Canada M5S 2S6
2250 Military Road, Tonawanda, N.Y. 14150-6000 U.S.A.

Distributors:
University of Toronto Press Distribution,
5201 Dufferin Street, Toronto (ON), Canada M3H 5T8

Gazelle Book Services, White Cross Mills, High Town,
Lancaster LA1 1XS U.K.

Independent Publishers Group,
814 N. Franklin Street, Chicago, Il. 60610 U.S.A.

First edition.
Printed in Canada.

Legal Deposit – Third Quarter
National Library of Canada
Library of Congress Catalog Card Number: 2005926036

Library and Archives Canada Cataloguing in Publication
Gasparini, Len
The broken world : poems, 1967-1998 / Len Gasparini.
(Essential poets series ; 132)
ISBN 1-55071-210-1
I. Title. II. Series.
PS8563.A7B76 2005   C811'.54   C2005-902555-7

Contents

6

In Memory of My Grandfather
Luigi Minello
(1876-1963)

Foreword

The first poetry I remember hearing as a child was Italian. My maternal grandfather was in the habit of reading aloud the *Divine Comedy* and the poems in *Il Crociato* – an Italian-Catholic newspaper to which he subscribed. I didn't know the language, but the poetic rhythms and my grandfather's soft musical voice were pleasing to my ear. Such was their sensory impact – a dance of language if you will – I am certain those sounds were imprinted on my subconscious.

This volume contains all the poems I wrote between 1967 and 1998 that I wish to preserve. They are taken from ten collections I published during that time. Some of the poems have been revised.

I believe a poet's business is to find his/her own rhythm and then find means to express that rhythm or verbal dance so that it interacts with the meaning of the poem. I have tried to render a poetic image of reality in rhymed verse, blank verse, and free verse.

The Roman poet Sextus Propertius wrote: *Non datur ad Musas currere lata via*. There is no royal road to poetry. In other words, you can't write about anything unless you've experienced it.

I wish to thank Antonio D'Alfonso (Guernica Editions) and the Ontario Arts Council for its generous support. As always, my heartfelt thanks to Leslie Thompson.

L.G.

The Photograph of My Grandfather
Reading Dante

Every evening
he would sit for hours
in his old wooden rocking chair,
with a glass of homemade red wine,
the *Divina Commedia* in his lap,
and a snuff-box on the table beside him.

Under a parchment-shaded floorlamp
that haloed his balding head
my mother's father, Luigi Minello,
would immerse himself in profundities.

And while the rest of our family played
cards or listened to the radio,
I would watch my grandfather
reading Dante *sotto voce*…
He was once photographed
without even knowing it.

Union Station, Toronto

Under black umbrellas
the bewildered immigrants
huddle together
holding their heavy luggage
in front of Union Station.

It's their first night
in a big strange city,
and even the rain is against them.

Cold-Water Flat Blues

With enough dimes to fill a mason jar
I fled the hollow-eyed specter
that haunted my homeless nights
sleeping in subways and laundromats,
and rented a cold-water flat.
Not bad for a start, eh? Now I can
endure my poverty in private.

Everything's OK save my landlord –
a parsimonious old bastard
if ever there was one – bored
with his pleurisy and widowerhood.

I wish I owned an escritoire.
Horace said poverty drove him to writing poetry.
A perpetual writer's cramp prevents me
from using toilet tissue properly.
The urine-yellow wallpaper was peeling,
so I covered the scabs with colorful maps
cut out of a stolen atlas.

I'm subsisting on tinned sardines,
apples, and peanut-butter sandwiches.
If I can't live like a king,
I'll certainly eat like one.

I was born under a falling star.
My only resources are a zip gun that shoots verbs;
a shiv that stabs aesthetically;
and brass-knuckled metaphors.
Now I'm ready to rob a public library,
kidnap some book publisher…
How else can a poet earn a living?

Self-Portrait, 1967

My fingers stampede the keyboard
Of a blue portable typewriter.
My poetry's the only thing I trust.
I pose as Melmoth the Wanderer
Steeped in mystery, violence, and lust.
I'm influenced by the moon,
But the sun is in my blood.
I have a wife, two kids, a steady job;
But I am most alive when buried
Deepest in the work I love.

Bela Lugosi

A pity you can't come back from the dead.
I've tried everything to evoke your spirit:
Seances, incantations, burnt offerings – everything.
I even bought a stuffed vampire bat
From a hunchbacked taxidermist.
I even sported a black cape.

But suppose you did appear.
What would my wife and children say?
Would they understand? Would you bite them?
No matter; my throat is bared.
I'd buy a one-way plane ticket
And fly with you to Transylvania.
We'd picnic in the moonlight,
Howl like werewolves, stay up all night
And have a bloody good time.

The Accident

His finger resembled
a crimson asparagus tip.
I was there, I saw the accident.
It happened on the night shift.

An electrician was trying
to loosen a jammed V-belt
by rotating the pulley
with his bare hand.

He was sweating and cursing.
I didn't know the motor was on.
The sudden whirring blur
of the V-belt startled me.

He didn't cry out but tried
to shake off his bloody hand.
His right index finger
was missing a knuckle.

I grabbed him before he fainted.
My stomach felt sick.
He was rushed to a hospital.

I keep seeing his finger
in my sleep. It resembles
a crimson asparagus tip.

Kilroy

Unmindful of the NO LOITERING sign
and the cop drinking coffee
in the Greyhound station restaurant,
a young man in black leather jacket,
Levi's and desert boots
leaned against a cigarette machine,
a cigarette hanging from his lips,
a defiant look on his face.

Ten minutes later the same cop
spotted the young man, checked his ID,
and told him to – "beat it
before I bust you for vagrancy."

O ubiquitous hipster,
you're too fuckin' cool and real
for this funky world, so beat it;
and with pen or penknife scrawl
whatever graffiti it takes to justify
your existence.

In Memory of the Empire Theatre

The Empire Theatre on Pitt Street is gone,
and with it the Saturday matinee movies
for us inner-city kids who grew up
aping the Bowery Boys' antics;
who thought the newsreel an intermission
so we could raise hell, laugh like Woody Woodpecker.
Saddlesore and trigger-happy, we trailed Hopalong Cassidy
into the black-and-white sunset.

It didn't matter the Empire Theatre
was a grungy old movie house
where it was rumored that rats roamed
among the spilled popcorn and jellybeans;
where some kid's fat head in front of us
kept getting in the way of our shoes;
where my pal Dicky Anderson always bought
a five-cent bag of peanuts,
and bit each one in half to make them last
through the double feature;
where an usher gave us the bum's rush
'cause we filched his flashlight
and filled it with tapwater;
where "Haber Boy" (who thought manual labor
was the name of a Mexican general)
did our mischievous bidding
if we promised him our empty pop bottles...

The Empire Theatre projected our youth
on its silver screen.
It was Sherwood Forest, Boot Hill, the Spanish Main...
When the wreckers scrapped the marquee
we knew it was curtains,
and tried to accept it like men
who have much of the boy in them.

Hart Crane

Hart Crane back from Marseilles where he had slept with his thirty sailors and he began again to drink Cutty Sark (the last bottle in the house).
Harry Crosby, *Shadows of the Sun*

Poems were bottles, bottles were sailors,
and Hart Crane bottled his genius
and drank it with good-looking sailors.
His mouth evaporated their voyages.

The displacement of his libido
listed the *S.S. Orizaba* to starboard.
He drank on deck – "O life's a geyser – "
cruised the foc's'le; painted Paris

a barroom-brawl red. The gendarmes
siphoned his soul with a rubber hose.
O broken bottles! O broken poems!
After such inspiration, what repose?

His mythic Bridge – aloft with seagulls –
gave breath to steel, rainbowed his spindrift song.
When he entered the broken world,
death, not love, permitted him voyage.

Anniversary Voyage

I feel like a swashbuckling buccaneer
beside you, and pretend I'm Errol Flynn
as we embark amid the cries of gulls
the ferryboat throbbing at the pier.
Certain sounds there are that steer a voyage out.

Believe me, love, I'd rather be aboard
a yacht, the nine Muses my only crew,
than sailing halfway across Lake Erie
to Pelee Island – to wander the sand beach,
birdwatch, swim, and make love al fresco.

With this ring, I willingly walked the plank,
served two years before the mast of marriage.
Now I watch the ferry's wake fanning out
over the lake. My perspective wavers.
I cherish the love; the promise I doubt.

Grapes

A nubile Italian girl
with purple-stained hands
is picking bunches of bloomy grapes,
filling wicker baskets with grapes.
The sun is shining,
and the boy working alongside her
is stripped to the waist.
All day in a Tuscan vineyard they work
in rhythm with the harvest.

From a hilltop church
the Angelus bell rings
across the terraced vineyards.
Evening's vine-tangled shadows
tempt the boy to steal a kiss.
The girl's face is light's last blush.

They walk away
toward their farmhouses in the hills.

At the supper table, after grace,
the full-bodied red wine
the girl's father pours
has the taste of the boy's lingering kiss.

Chinatown Nocturne

Unshaven, trench-coated, with hat
slouched over one eye, like Bogart,
and sweaty hand on blackjack,
I stand under a pagoda neon sign,
wondering whether I should roll a drunk
or mug a dragon. The night is foggy…
I reach for a cigarette. Behind me,
Charlie Chan strikes a match.

Tunnel Bus to Detroit

From downtown Windsor
it's a five-minute bus ride
under the river
to dynamic Detroit.
On weekdays the bus is crowded
with young secretaries.
I politely proffer my seat,
peruse a newspaper,
and pretend not to notice
their long nyloned legs,
the way they look –
so chic and sophisticated,
dressed for romance instead of work.
But who am I fooling?
Who knows? I could be
an escaped sex maniac
commuting incognito;
a white-collar *frotteur*
carrying a black leather briefcase.
And what if the bus broke down?
the lights went out?
the tunnel sprang a leak?
With civil intent, I dream
of improving their careers
in five frenzied minutes.

Kafka's Other Metamorphosis

Franz Kafka had a nightmare
that he was a butterfly brooch
fastened to the low-necked dress
of some whore slurping cabbage soup.

He suddenly fell kerplunk
into that bowl of boiled kraut.
He did not drown but awoke
as a pale green caterpillar

and was gobbled up. *Mein Gott!*
The whore contracted syphilis,
and had a chancre the size
of a chrysalis on her twat.

Pickup

He followed me into a bar
out of the neon night rain
and sat down beside me.
Suspicious, I pegged him as a weirdo
slumming for kinky sex.
I ordered a stinger.
He asked for the same.
Our eyes met in the bar mirror
for a frozen moment.
A reefer broke the mirror's ice
when he gave me a light.
He came on like Peter Lorre, camping it up;
claimed he worked "in theatre";
off-Broadway, of course...
a designer of stage sets,
makeup man, or whatever.
I told him my business
was minding my own.
He bought me a drink.
I wondered what his proposition would be.
He was sizing me up.
We finally left the bar together –
pusher and buyer; a butch fag
and a pickup in drag.

Imagine our bewilderment when
(with handcuffs ready)
we simultaneously produced ID's
proving we were plainclothesmen.
There are eight million stories
in the naked city.
This has been one of them.

On Being Introduced to Irving Layton at a Literary Soirée

The room was full of academics
mixing prose with gin.
Irving Layton was guest of honor.
He wore a wolfish grin.

Several CanLit profs were present.
"Priapic best describes his verse."
"He called Northrop Frye a eunuch."
I heard the lionized poet curse.

We shook hands. He asked me what
I didn't do for a living.
(I'd no invisible means of support.)
"Write poetry when I'm not driving —"

And he, misunderstanding: "Any luck?"
"Writing a sestina," I said,
"is like trying to haul a bunch
of jackrabbits on a flatbed truck."

1967

Grandfather Clock

O thou weight-driven, coffinlike grotesquery,
With unseen shackles for thy maker,
I'm the one who gave thee the time of day.
What clock-faced, pendulum-tongued monster
Have I created, that now chimes my life away?

The Houseplants

The houseplants (begonias, geraniums,
African violets) to which you gave
so much of your time and care
soon wilted after you left me.

Distressed by your absence,
our unpleasant break, I thought
of myself in relation to them.
They needed water, I needed you.

Now that I've grown accustomed
to their showy green handshake,
they remind me of the love I took
for granted when you were here.

Valentine

A razorsharp wind
shaves the snowlathered roofs
of passing cars.

Holding my heart
in my gloved hands,
I enter a barbershop.

The barber
(whose frigid wife
I once seduced on a bet)
slits my throat
with an icicle.

If you visit his barbershop,
you'll see a real valentine:
my heart in formaldehyde.

Written on a Paper Napkin

The snow falling outside
a restaurant window this morning
mocks my appetite with each spoonful
of cornflakes I lift to my mouth.

Yesterday she undid
her ribboned bundle of love letters,
sneered – *Such nice penmanship you have*,
and tore up my letters, one by one.
Mute, I watched her hands
making the room cold.

The snow falling outside
a restaurant window this morning…

Yesterday I should have –
I should have said something cruelly apropos;
but the engagement ring on her wormwhite finger
contained my hate in embryo.

Subversion

We bravely shoulder the signs of the times –
signs that shout – MAKE LOVE NOT WAR.
But isn't this slogan paradoxical,
like fighting for peace,
when it still takes two to tango,
and hate is the aphrodisiac of the people?
Man has made war through the ages.
That's why the world's overpopulated.

Two native Austrians, Freud and *"der Fuhrer,"*
shook hands in their sleep.
Perhaps the significant years of their deaths
should have been reversed.
One made history a front for human nature;
the other gave human nature a face.

Universal love would breed
annihilation, a rosy doom.
Come, let us love one another
slowly, slowly to death.

Soul Poem

they live on the dole
his wife turns tricks
their kids found a dead rat
in the toilet bowl
and he'd sell his soul
to see LeRoi Jones
enter a Southern Baptist church
on Christmas day, stroll
up the main aisle to the altar,
fingersnap the sign of the cross, and holler:
HEY, WHITEY!
DON'T JUST HANG THERE!
SMILE! IT'S YOUR BIRTHDAY!

Artist's Model

Just the way you sit
on that plum-colored sofa,
with your legs crossed,
sipping a cocktail
is enough to make me forget
my family, job,
and finance company.

When you shift the weight
of your gluteus maximus
from one leg to the other,
I can hear the nylon susurrus
of your thighs
scissoring
your voluptuous mons veneris.

I could possess your essence
by painting you;
but heaven it would be
to paint your essence
in my mind
while possessing you.
Art has an alternative, too.

Nude on a Motorcycle

O what equestrienne is this
who burlesques both myth and metaphor
astride a souped-up centaur?
Her white skin is sleeker than chrome.
Does she ride a motorcycle
or a motorcyclone?
Beside her, Lady Godiva
would have feigned saddle sore.
In the name of pop art,
paste her bare ass on a billboard.

The Eavesdropper

A strange voice is conversing
with another strange voice
on a telephone party line.
The receiver is stuck to my ear.
A man and a woman are exchanging confidences.
I feel like I'm a priest in a confessional.
My hands and ears are sweating.
Silence is the best listener.
(A dial tone is such a lonely sound.)
Do they detect my breathing?
Do I dare to interject?
Maybe we could make a threesome.
My involvement's purely vicarious.
I am the voyeur's doppelganger.
I am your darkest secret. I have connections.

Truckstop Blues

I drive a big eighteen-wheeler,
I live day and night on the road,
Washing down bennies with coffee,
Deadheading or hauling a load.

A Mack bulldog is my mascot.
There's diesel fuel in my blood.
I love the hiss of the air brakes,
The horsepower under the hood.

Once upon a time and a half
I jack-knifed my tractor-trailer
And walked away without a scratch
But looking a whole lot paler.

I once picked up a wendigo
Outside Wawa, Ontario;
Said she'd give head if I let her
Sing on my CB radio.

On the nod one night at the wheel
(A case of highway hypnosis),
I thought I was driving uphill;
That straightaway seemed damned endless.

There's a coop a half mile ahead,
And my logbook is way behind.
Although I'm a bit overweight,
I can stop my rig on a dime.

I drive a big eighteen-wheeler.
I'm up to my neck in arrears.
As long as I keep on trucking,
My life is the shifting of gears.

Solo

The audience sat entranced
listening to Snooks wail on sax
at Antonelli's Place.
I was with my date. She wanted to dance;
but that mean tenor sax
took up all the space.

I Was a Poet for the Mafia

It pays to have relatives in Cicero
Who mean business in Chicago,
And connections in Detroit
Who make book for the big publishers
in New York and Toronto.

My typewriter was gunmetal gray
And deadly portable.
Its hair trigger inspired my finger.
I forget the actual number of editors
Slumped over desks, pumped full of poems.
Rejection slips were their death warrants.
They didn't understand
Poetry was a front
For the back of my hand.

I collaborated with torpedoes
Who were the avant-garde
In their profession;
Attended literary parleys
In sunny hiding places,
Like Miami, Las Vegas, Palermo.
I lived high and fine,
And never had a deadline.
My books made the WANTED list.
I was quoted on police line-ups
By suspects who knew my poems by heart.

The critics tried to convict me,
But my agent happened to be
A syndicate lawyer with pull.
With the power of the poem,
I became as infamous as Capone.

Alas! I learned too late that vice
Paid worse than verse
When a bullet obliterated my poetry.
I was a poet for the Mafia.
Bury me in Sicily.

Solitary Confinement

My prison cell is my naked self.
I am immured in the mirrored space
Between time and eternity.
In my cell, everything is the center
Of everything else.
My navel is the universe.
I do not serve time, time serves me.
The turnkey cannot enter my kingdom.

In Memory of a Nun

In the evening, after prayer,
she goes for a solitary stroll –
shadowlike, grey-veiled, with head bowed –
fingering a black rosary.

Through the convent garden she strolls,
whispering *Ave Marias.*
A fragrant breeze ruffles her habit.
She pauses to smell a rose.

The grey-veiled nun has a vision
of love incarnate in Christ:
the darkness deep down inside the rose,
to which the bloom is sacrificed.

The Buffalo Nickel

Hitchhiking in the cold prairie wind,
he fumbled in his pockets
for change; took out two dimes,
some pennies, and a nickel.

For the first time he studied the nickel
and understood his situation.

Of his once proud heritage,
when grasses and wildflowers
tickled the bellies of the buffalo,
only symbols remained.

Let the wind blow, he thought;
the coins would buy him a cup of coffee.

Up the road was a gas station-diner.
He hunched toward it.
A sign in the window said –
We dont serv injuns.

In the Ward

The night wind gnawed at the straitjacket
of sleep. In the ward,
a barefoot woman was droning nursery rhymes.
A dream escaped down the corridor.

The figure lay strapped to his cot
below a barred moonlit window;
said he was "listening to the susurrus of ailanthus leaves."
Their shadows on the bare wall
quivered like yard-long centipedes.
A sudden fear horripilated him.
Or was it DTs?

The night nurse on the intercom
summoned two orderlies.
Mother Goose piped in: "Paraldehyde
tastes better after brushing with Colgate."

Cocktail

A slice of sunset
salutes her lips
across a glass lagoon.

If I were a skindiver
for one tropic evening,
I'd kiss that mermaid's
maraschino moon.

Greasy Spoon Blues

Gus the Greek is a short-order cook
in a greasy spoon on Bloor Street.
He came to Canada in 1964,
thinking the streets were paved with gold.

After work, Gus drinks retsina
in his furnished room (when homesick,
he plays the bouzouki and sings
bawdy Greek songs), then he wears out

the night prowling the taverns in search
of women lonely as he. "In Greece,"
says Gus, "there's a joy of living.
Here we put all our trust in banks."

Gus keeps worry beads in his room.
Late at night he lingers over a mug
of coffee in some greasy spoon —
smoking, staring blankly into space.

The Garret

My black cat meows to be let out.
It is a foggy autumn night –
a night for smoking sweet hashish
and making love by candlelight.

To control the passage of time,
the author of *Les Fleurs du Mal*
removed the hands from his clock
and on its dial wrote: *It is later than you think*.

Why do I feel a sudden nostalgia
for the garret I lived in long ago?
I was jobless then, and directionless;
but I could really rock and roll.

Hometown

O the ineffable joy
of returning to my hometown
after so many years away.
The train crawled into the station on time.
A pale winter sun came out to greet me.
I wanted to shake hands with the world.
Who said you can't go home again?
To celebrate my homecoming,
I took a taxi to my favorite tavern.
Everything was copasetic, A-OK,
as we used to say in the sixties.
I quaffed a carafe of Chardonnay,
tipped the homely waitress a fin,
and swaggered to the men's room.
On the wall, above a stained urinal
choked with cigarette filters,
some Kilroy of graffiti had scrawled:
If you have only a year to live,
spend it in Windsor
and it'll seem like twenty.

The Mannequin

As I walked past a display window
Late one night, on the make,
A well-dressed mannequin
Winked at me me.
I did a double take.

She pressed her lips against the glass
But left no breath.
Soundless words she mouthed.
I felt like a ventriloquist
On a street of death.

Humanly alone and desperate
For one euphoric kiss,
I smashed the glass
And ravished her...
And they locked me up for this.

At the Golden Dragon

And while we dined on moo koo gai kew
and other unpronounceable dishes
the waiter served us oolong tea
in cups the size of a Pekin's egg.

Unable to read the tea leaves
we cracked open our fortune cookies
looking to find some Asian wisdom
worthy of Confucius and Charlie Chan.

They read: *Success lies close to home*
and *You will have strong artistic instincts*.
We tipped the waiter... we hurried home...
we didn't go outdoors for a week.

Epitaph for Emily Carr

Here lies Emily Carr –
green thumb and artist.
With one brushstroke
she planted a forest.

Trophies

Shouts, laughter, *I double-dare you* ring out,
as my two children see who can catch
the most tadpoles in the willow-shaded creek
behind my father's cottage.

All morning they explore a jungle
of giant ragweeds
where imaginary monsters abound;
come back raccoon-faced from their safari
and primitivize the den with pinecones,
wildflowers, insects in glass jars…
trophies of a summer day.

That was seventeen summers and three divorces ago.
Memory is seeing who we are
alter who we were.
The future looms ghostly.

With my Swiss army knife,
I extract a tooth from an alligator dead
on the roadside in the Florida Everglades.
Today is my daughter's wedding day.

Pelee Island Spring

Dawn disperses the misty stillness.
The island's east shore is focused
with clamshells, pebbles, driftwood,
spotted sandpipers teetering along.

Sunlight spreads the horizon
across Lake Erie's glistening lens
whose latitude gulls reflect
like keen white pennants.

Out of the mist the island rises.
Tall trees, throbbing with birds,
sweeten the green air
as spring plants it feet in the earth.

Pelee Island Autumn

The map's legend... Hulda's Rock,
Vin Villa, the island's limestone ruins...
and the lake washing its hands
in the blood of an Indian sunset.

The rain ripens these perspectives –
the harvest of a painter's eye.
To ponder them is to unearth
the archives of another autumn.

A skein of wild geese skims across the sky.
The foliage flushes, pheasant-hued.
Dogs and the guns of hunters
bark, echo, bark in the distance.

Old Lighthouse, Pelee Island

Straying from the island's east road,
I picked my way through underbrush
and came upon a wild strip of beach.
Gulls took wing at my approach.

The sunlit mist on the waveless lake
slowly revealed a water snake
swimming close to shore. I walked the beach
past Lizard Point, in step with the solitude.

Haunted-looking even in daylight,
an old lighthouse of weathered limestone
towered beaconless above
a reedy marsh athrob with blackbirds.

Through an opening I crept inside.
Among cobwebs, dust, and shadows
a decrepit staircase blindly spiraled.
To the very top I climbed.

Atop the ruined lighthouse I stood,
and saw it in an earlier light,
when storms, fog, and fogbound ships
were but reflections of its unending day.

Pumpkins

Under the harvest moon
a pumpkin patch glistens with dew
where a shadowy scarecrow stands.

On yellow-flowered vines
that trail along the ground,
the bee-pollinated pumpkins ripen
until the ground bulges
with orange rotundities
the wind cannot budge.

The witchery of Halloween,
the alchemy of autumn,
turn pumpkins into pies
and leering jack-o'-lanterns.

Essex County Pastoral

Where the dirt road narrows
to a tractor's width, a shrubby field,
sheeted in mist, stretches lakeward.

A weedy ditch crawls alongside a split-rail fence.
On decaying tree stumps mushrooms cluster.
The staghorn sumac is red.

In a corner of the field
an abandoned harrow
rusts on its disks.

Under the autumn sky
a grove of aspens
yellows the flat countryside.

The field, the cloudy morning surround
a wheelrut filled with rainwater
from which a crow is drinking.

Erie Beach

A rotting carp cast ashore
by the waves.

A sand-filled Coke bottle
jutting out of the sand.

A shiny clamshell,
some weathered driftwood,

and, if you look closely,
the rubber ring of a condom

lying beside a child's
naked doll in the weeds.

At Raymond Knister's Grave

For Myrtle Grace

An inland gull wheeled overhead.
Lake Erie was a country mile from where we stood –
Myrtle, my wife and I –
In a landscape reserved for the dead.

And while we stood at his graveside,
Joined together by something more intimate
Than hands, time seemed suspended
Like a tree standing in its own shadow.

We could not bury the day by brooding
On the dead. It was a May afternoon.
The mist-green countryside bloomed.
I read aloud the poem engraved

On his blue marble gravestone.
After a silence we walked silently away,
Knowing that change is unchangeable
And beyond wondering about.

Weeds

Long live the weeds...

Gerard Manley Hopkins

Weeds seem to multiply overnight.
Although we hoe or uproot by hand
the common and the troublesome ones,
still they survive the hoe, the herbicide,
holding their ground as though they own it:
disfiguring our lawns, suffocating our flowers,
thriving even in crevices of concrete.
It's not their appearance offends us,
but lack of cultivation, the vigorousness
with which they invade our gardens.
Yet who are we to deny them wild growth?
For once let us spare their weedy lives,
let us call them by their proper names:
lady's thumb, toadflax, shepherd's-purse, goldenrod...

Field Trip

In nature, nothing is wasted.
Stumbling over
an old mossed log in the forest,
my son discovers its underside
half buried in humus
teeming with fungi, seedlings, insects...
and is amazed by the life
its decay has created.

Detroit Nocturne

From a tenement rooftop
a black boy watches
the total eclipse of the moon
and spits watermelon seeds at the stars.

Raymond Souster's Toronto

Waiting at a red light
early this morning
at King and Bathurst streets,
I see a ragged wino
asleep on the sidewalk,
a stray dog sniffing at him,
in front of the Wheat Sheaf Tavern.
On the tavern's mansard roof
a signboard reads –
EVEN DIRTY OLD MEN NEED LOVE

Junkball

For Ted Plantos

When the last batter struck out,
dozens of autograph hounds
ran in pursuit of their quarry
who had just pitched a no-hitter.
One of them, an ex-junkie
whose pockmarked face was familiar,
moved in for the kill.
He carried no autograph book but himself.
Removing his sunglasses,
he accosted the pitcher:
"Son, with an arm like yours
I could've had a picnic!"

The Escapist

I want
to leave
an endless
trail of
picture
postcards
behind
me.

The Book Reviewer

In my study – snug as a monk's cell –
the mushroom-colored walls are bookends.
Here one can read the smell of books –
books I've praised or panned in book reviews
the past fifteen hack-written years.

Breathing my blurbs and squibs,
the paper ghosts of authors haunt this room.
They stand or lie dog-eared and badly thumbed.
Some rub shoulders with the classics.
Some plots are predictable as a nun's period.
After all has been said, and all *has* been said,
the worse book is no book at all.

Knisteresque

The leaves rust and fall,
rust and fall in an old orchard
wet with the dew of dawn.
The grazing cattle tread
on sweetly rotting windfalls.
The veins of the earth
soak up the season's cider.

If Love Is Heaven

Gabriele d'Annunzio, "the faun of the Abruzzi,"
deflowered God's angels with his genius.
He employed the words of the spirit
to obtain the works of the flesh.

If love is heaven, why does a man weary
of fucking his beloved, or a woman angle
for some womanizer's penis?
Heaven knows I've been there – four times married.

We crave love but live with less
in the abstract climate of the heart.
There is no evil so great
that love cannot accommodate.

Son and Stepson

Both of them are mirrors
waiting for me
to break in half.

I cannot look at one
without seeing
the other's reflection.

My gaze encloses them
like an aquarium,
through which they peer.

They are my eyes
looking back at me
in two different colors.

In their eyes I see myself
divided by love,
blinded by guilt.

Adult Entertainment

In the smoky, musty darkness
of an X-rated movie house,
three men are having sex with a woman
on the screen. There is a tremor
of genitals, like sea anemones
waving their tentacles.

Breathing vicariously, the audience watches
this stark abstraction of flesh.
Each voyeur seems lost in himself –
a shadow that squints through a keyhole.

Lust slithers at their feet.
The swollen darkness crouches like a cave.
When the houselights come on,
the audience stumbles to the nearest exit.

Museum Piece

How painstakingly
they try to camouflage
the ithyphallic satyr
with a fig leaf

until, frustrated,
they have to lop off his lust
balls and all
for public display.

Alter Ego

For D.S.

"Let it rain – I'm going to the Orient,"
said my alter ego.
"No matter where you go there you are," said I.
He went to Mexico.

His journey was existential.
He turned his back on himself
and drove thousands of miles
only to stumble on his shadow

holed up in a seaport slum
with some fourteen-year-old *puta*,
the crabs, and a worm
in an empty mescal bottle.

Through strange cities he passed alone,
doubting his own identity,
discarding it piecemeal
until he felt weightless, giddy.

The postcards he mailed to his estranged wife
bore cryptic messages
that read like graffiti.
She brooded over their meaning.

One night in Cincinnati,
totally stoned, he took a room
in a run-down hotel, and killed cockroaches
the size of a man's thumb.

"I trust all joy!" he shouted,
quoting Roethke, and stopped his car
to watch the sun rising above
the Great Smokies.

At a private exhibition of still lifes –
forbidden fruit unframed –
he drank bloody Marys with a naked ex-nun
in her Stewart Street atelier.

"The people I like are the people
I become like," said D.S. to his double,
who said "With schizophrenia you're never alone."
Reality made him risk enchantment.

In a Nogales, Arizona disco
he danced a peyote dance,
and beheld Isis lifting her veil.
Away she spirited him –

all the way to Montreal
where he rented a flat in a cul-de-sac,
sold his car, read the *Bhagavad-Gita*,
and fathered a bastard.

In the rainy night of his soul
he experienced a vision.
It was as if his life had been painted
and the colors had run.

High Park

When you left me
you took everything
except the echo
of your good-bye.

The nights of love
still toss our shadows
naked as the moon
across the floor.

Divorce Court

Here the air is inflammable.
The black-robed judge wears a death's-head mask.
The lawyers sit like precision instruments under glass.
Their clients are knives and forks.
Their clients are knives and forks.
Here marriages are dismembered, disremembered.
And divorce is the door prize.

After the Divorce

After the divorce
the ground walks on you
for a while.

It is not the world
that is upside down,
it is your head.

You consult a psychiatrist.
The psychiatrist is a woman
from Iceland.
You unburden yourself.
She looks at her wristwatch,
removes her glasses, and says:
"Whatever your priorities are."

You pop a Valium
and feel its white fuzz
floating your nerves
like tiny parachutes.

You see your children once a month,
if you are lucky.
They seem like lost playmates
from your own childhood.
You borrow them
to practise playing father.

When you run into friends,
you feel like a burglar
who has dropped his flashlight.
You pretend. They pretend.
You abscond with your guilt.

You smell her absence
and touch yourself
like a blind man.
You are lonely.
Even the food you eat
tastes lonely.

You switch on the radio
and listen to music
till her image darkens
and it is total night
inside you.

Part of you is buried in her.
Part of her is buried in you.
Each of you is a grave for the other.

You live with a woman.
She has a son.
He reminds you of your son.
You run away.

You live with another woman.
She has a son.
You remind him of his father.
He wants to run away.

At night you lie awake
and breathe love
into the emptiness beside you.
You give it a shape.
You make it real.

In the morning,
you wake up wifeless
and find yourself
on the wrong side
of the dream.

The Fatherless Child

I remember the fatherless child
whose mother I slept with
for two lost, guilt-haunted years;
the child who craved a father
while I suffered the absence
of my own children, having left them
so I could live with the child's mother.

I remember chancing upon him
in a playground one bright summer day
long after his mother and I had parted.
He used to be my father, said the child
to his playmate on the swing.
Ah, in that moment I never felt
more like a father to him.

Separated

Separated from you by an act
Of my own choosing, and the misery
Of a broken marriage – a marriage
Whose sacrament had become a syndrome,

I picture you now, Elizabeth,
A young girl in a white spring dress,
Reading a book of fairy tales
On your eleventh birthday.

What is memory but an emotion
On vacation. Your image inhabits me
Like a mirror in an empty room.
Your beginning was once upon a time.

Is it for this your blameless absence
Suspends me like a bell?
My heart could be that bell
ringing, ringing, ringing…

I remember reading *Rapunzel* to you
In our make-believe forest tower,
When the night wind was the Wicked Witch
And the magic word was Daddy.

Of redemption I sing, O my daughter.
If love is the beginning,
Let us begin to understand the end;
Then love can live happily ever after.

Adultery

Although adultery sounds biblical,
and guilt is masochism with a halo,
you begin to wonder if lust was worth
the shame, the deceit, the anger
that undermined your marriage;
you begin to wonder how your conscience
covered up the affairs, the pickups
who inspired one madrigal too many,
which you didn't sing but whispered in the dark
of your heart, in a room by the hour.
You go on wondering till it happens
again, like a slow-motion flashback,
remembering Saint Augustine's words:
"Lord, make me chaste – but not yet."

Leftover Love to Kill

For S.

It's strange how you remember the little things,
the things that didn't seem significant then:
the bag of cherries you surprised her with
when she was painting a house porch;
the birdlike way she fluttered her hands,
as if trying to escape from the cage of her body
to embrace a feeling purer than alpine air;
the ivy leaf she used as a bookmark;
the tears she planted like seeds
when you moved your typewriter to another city...
all the little things
that snuggled up to your heart
while your blood tingled with music,
and crickets stopped their mating to listen...
the things that seem significant now.

And now you are left with a love
torturously rooted in light.
You are left with a memory of love
that bites like a diamond.
But how do you kill it?

You could break the necks of a thousand tulips.
You could fall in love with yourself
and hate her for it.
You could turn your back on your shadow.
You could fill the infinite space between two stars
with a poem that never sleeps.
But what would you do with the ashes?

Valentine's Day 1978

Detroit Revisited

For Salvatore Ala

On a decaying street corner,
a few doors beyond
an X-rated cinema's
orgy of neon,
stands a statuesque black hooker
with a blonde wig on.

Hardcore

On a Detroit street that knew no daylight,
black hookers slouched in doorways, waiting.
The headlights of curb-cruising cars were moons
with hard-ons. When a car stopped, voices muttered:
How much? Regular or French? Around the world.
To the honkey trick – horny yet nervous,
whose first time it was on John R. Street,
some shadow sweating strong perfume would purr:
My big red lips can make a rose
on the end of your hard white stem.
But if you tried to embrace her
she would suddenly turn sassy, and sneer:
You're not here to make love, you've here to fuck!
And you'd wonder about that for a long time.

Nymphomania

The very word is like a spell
compelling all manner of men
to think with their bodies
and dance the dance of Shiva.

Mention the word, nymphomania,
and a strange sensation grips
the testicles, like a parachute jump
before the chute opens.

How many women who use the sorcery
of their sex to enslave a man
in the chains of his jism
would rather fuck than eat?

How many men would marry a nympho?
How many men – cloven-hoofed,
in stud, from studying *Playboy* –
secretly have womb envy?

This is the chimera reported
in part by Kinsey *et al*.
Its symbol is a symptom:
an erotic erosion of nerves.

Belle River Pearl was a local legend
when I was a horny adolescent.
Biology's got us by the gonads.
Too much is never enough.

On Yonge Street

In a strip joint on Yonge Street
a man in a grimy raincoat
was nursing a pink lady.
Alone he sat, making wet sucking sounds
with his mouth and fingers,
absorbing each bump and grind,
wallowing in legs, buttocks, breasts
until his whole being was buried
under that avalanche of flesh.

And when the music stopped,
and a stripper strutted past his table –
O if he could have crawled
into her cunt and died…
He spilled his pink lady.

Toronto Nocturne

Unable to sleep,
he chain-smokes through the night.
The wild insomniac inside him
is on another binge.

From his high-rise balcony,
he looks at the street below,
and feels the dizzy fear
of simply letting go.

One April night he fell four stories,
and landed on a green lawn;
suffered a nosebleed, a chill.
At Mount Sinai Hospital,

a physician said:
"It's a miracle he's alive."
Actually, it was Valium and beer;
but that's another story.

"If dying is an art – "
to quote a lady who knew,
an artist is the suicide
who decides not to –

Rereading Kerouac's *On the Road*

I leave the squares, the straights, the bourgeoisie
Behind me. I romance the road again.
The ghosts are there, the neon midnights too.
Wine-Spodee-o-Dee! Hallelujah, I'm a bum!
The great adventure isn't being there
But *getting there* – CHOOSE YOUR RUT CAREFULLY,
YOU'LL BE IN IT FOR A LONG TIME. Burma-Shave.
The blonde waitress in the all-night diner
Looks naked even with her clothes on.
Yaaaaaheee! I won't settle down till I die.
 – And the sad exhilaration of being rootless
And alone, going somewhere, anywhere.

Streets

There are streets that follow us
wherever we go; streets
that run our lives day after day;
streets that corner us at night
when we are lonely or alone;
and there are streets that get lost, too.

Fire and Ashes

In Memoriam: Marcel Horne

The last time I saw Marcel Horne
he was holed up in a Toronto rooming house
in the dead of winter, waiting
for a driveaway going to Florida,
where he hoped to rekindle his past
as *El Diablo* – the Firebreather.

I marveled how he lived as a carny
out of an old battered trunk the size of a truck.
From country to country he wandered
with his Swiss passport and fireproof lungs.
The only thing stationary about him
was his post-office box.

I first met him at a New Year's Eve party.
Between tokes of Acapulco gold
he laughed bitterly that his book
Annals of the Firebreather,
which I'd praised in a review,
was banned in his hometown.

Built like a bouncer in a clip joint,
he had a hustler's streetwise look.
Hey, rube, under which shell's the pea?
His life was a psychedelic sideshow,
and the colored capsules he took
dissolved the alienation he felt.

When he performed his fire act
to "Third Stone from the Sun,"
he'd slip into a yogic trance
of total concentration;
drink gasoline from a brass cup,
hold a torch to his mouth
and blow a flame twenty feet long,
as an offering to the Cosmic God of Unity.

"The best thing about life," he said,
"is that you never know
what is going to happen next."
In the orange-blossom fragrance
of a Florida night,
he was killed by a hit-and-run driver.

I heard he was cremated;
but I not so sure of that.
If I knew Marcel,
it was all part of his act.

Dream

In my dream, I clung to a broken spar,
half-naked, shipwrecked, and weary;
helpless as that sea turtle I saw overturned
behind some flyblown cantina,
its gashed neck bleeding.
A tropic sun blazed down
till sky and sea were one.
Did my aloneness and fear of drowning
project the head of a swimming tiger?
A tiger swimming in circles?
What fabulous beast, what sea-born sphinx
was this before me? what strange omen?
The tiger swam round and round,
then glided toward me like a phantom.
We sensed each other's fear.
When the tiger clawed for the spar,
our survival seemed uncertain.
I swear I saw the human in its eyes.
Perhaps it saw the wild animal in mine.

Logos Bogus

In the beginning was the Whore,
and the Whore was with child,
and the child was stillborn,
and darkness held dominion over all.

Then came the Word,
and the Word was Love incarnate,
and Love was the light of the world
shining in darkness.

Is not the light darkness invisible?
Is not the essence of God
the nature of man who created God
in his own image?

What fish ever breathed holy water,
that my seed could swim
in the womb-tomb of night?
What serpent-entwined tree and dollar sign

could infuse my soul with the knowledge
of Good and Evil?
I cannot say, or guess, for I know
only a grave beside a garden,

where the moon gapes, and the fir tree
grows taller than Christmas,
the owl goes hungry, and we
become as fertilizer after death.

Dirge for Janis Joplin

It wasn't her soul
but the *woman* inside her soul
who screamed *Get it while you can*
when she sang of love.

We listened to the music
devouring her alive
till she became a thing
inhabited by a cry.

Offstage her pain was such
that she reached
for a needle
to stanch the bleeding.

Alleluia!

1

We stand, we sit, we kneel, we pray
among the multitude of worshipers
in the gothic basilica of Our Lady.
It is Easter Sunday. Christ has risen again
from the dead. Alleluia!
White candles and lilies adorn the altar.
A priest in white vestments
is celebrating the Mass in Latin.
In nomine Patris, et Filii, et Spiritus Sancti.
The life-sized crucifix, statues of saints, incense, holy water,
and the stained-glass windows depicting the Passion
infuse our hearts with faith, which is the evidence
of things unseen; hope in God's Word;
and charity – the greatest of these.
Kyrie eleison. Kyrie eleison. Kyrie eleison.
Glorifying the triune God,
the choir soars in the summit of Heaven.
Alleluia! Alleluia! Alleluia!
The ritual magnifies the Lord.
Our spirits rejoice in the Father Almighty.
Meekly we accept the Mysteries
that burn reason at the stake
with cloven tongues of fire.

2

When I was a child, I did not put away childish things.
(I was fond of playing with toy soldiers.)
When I made my First Communion, I was careful not to bite
the consecrated bread, or glorified body of Christ,
fearing he would bleed to death in my mouth.
Agnus Dei, qui tollis peccata mundi, miserere nobis.

Although our fear of hell is irrational,
we pray for deliverance from evil
and hope to attain the kingdom of God.
Lulled by the sacred liturgy,
we partake of the Sacrifice of the Mass and are forgiven.
Anus Dei, qui tollis peccata mundi, dona nobis pacem.

3

Is not the light darkness invisible?
Can good exist without evil?
Perhaps religion is a refuge from death,
because death seems too final
for *Homo* sap – the absurd animal.

O Christ, come down from the Cross;
come down from the Cross,
and throw in the vinegar-soaked sponge.
Call us cowards, sycophants, hypocrites...
We created God in our own image.
O darkness invisible.
Immortality is for the living.
You live for us with your dying.
Without *Homo sap* there would be no religion.
Without religion there would be no God.
If there were no God...
We do not believe. We fear.

Love Poem

You are pregnant with love,
and it truly becomes you,
like a conch shell whispering the sea's secret.

You are a sweet mushroom
in the meadow of my right hand,
and soft as the dew on a rabbit's nose.

Alone, you are a moon
without light, an empty vase,
a ripe breast crying for a mouth to feed.

You are the prime mover
of my metaphors.
And when our bodies speak, our minds listen.

Azaleas for an Outpatient

Around you the hospital whitely blooms.
Under the anesthetic
your veins are a maze of red and blue tunnels
through which you wander, lost.

You are a garden in winter.
The gynecologist will see to it
that your garden is flowerless in spring.

Your tubes are tied; the D and C is done.
No more condoms, no more pills,
no more nursery rhymes...

I thought of your tubal ligation,
of the azaleas I gave you –
pink, fragrantless azaleas –
so named because they flourish in dry soil,
like metaphors for modern love.

Indian Serenade

For Lynda

From a train window she watched the sunset
crimsoning the May sky.
The boreal forest of the Canadian Shield streamed by.
What her thoughts were then I could only guess.
She looked pensive,
as though where she was going
held less glamor
than from where she was coming.
(A beautiful woman traveling alone
is never alone for long.)

I gazed at the darkening landscape
and imagined myself pan-frying rainbow trout
over a brushwood fire,
with her clad in buckskin beside me.
(Those lakes, forests and rocky hills went unnoticed
until the Group of Seven painted them.)

On an eastbound train
in that wolf-haunted wilderness,
what could I do, what could I do
but cast a spell to possess her spirit,
and call down the thunder
to fatten the rock-ribbed land with rain.

Shore Leave

I sit in a room in Tijuana,
watching a woman undress.
Wavelets of clothing pool at her feet.

Peering at a tank of tropical fish,
a white cat purrs in my lap
as I stroke its head and supple spine.

The woman is bathed in candlelight.
On her left buttock
floats a seahorse tattoo.

Like cream pouring out of a pitcher,
the cat uncurls and stretches,
digging its claws into my summer whites.

Around the room the woman dances,
dripping with jewelry,
allowing herself to be adored.

For twenty U.S. dollars
you can ride her *caballito de mar*.
The cat leaps from my lap to the floor.

Full Moon

Like the moon,
you have journeyed alone from afar
into your ninth month.

Sometimes at night when you are sleeping,
I touch the firm warm fullness of your pregnancy,
and my hand glows.
And sometimes at night when the Pacific tide tiptoes to our
    door,
I think of the ripe fetus that floats
in the moon of your belly.

To My Newborn Son

Born December 9, 1981

I hold you – wet from your mother's womb.
You breathe, brightening the room
With your birth-light; you cry,
And color the air with your cries.
You are a bright new arrow
For the bow of Sagittarius.
Life be your target, my son.

British Columbia

The sun cut itself
on a mountain peak, and bled
into the valley.

Devil's Club

In the rain forest there is a shrub
called devil's club, *Oplopanax horridus*,
a ginseng-related shrub so spiny
it cannot grow without pricking itself.

Hikers fear the plant's horrid weaponry.
The stalk and branchlets bristle with spines
needle-sharp. Even the leaves are spiny –
on both sides; and the bloodred berries,

relished by bears, are poisonous.
A hardy shrub, ten feet or more in height.
When the spines puncture the flesh they sting
and sting and, unless removed at once,

work inward like porcupine quills.
They fester if embedded in the skin.
I brushed a spine against my thumb.
The small wound bothered me for three days.

On the northwest coast, Indians believe
the devil's club has magical powers.
Medicinal it is. They brew tea
from the bitter inner bark as a tonic.

An Indian guilty of breaking a taboo
was first stripped naked, and then heaved
into a dense thicket of devil's club.
It makes a handsome garden ornamental.

Haiku for a Sperm Whale

Seed within a womb
of a womb that is the sea.
A whale is God's heart.

Fog in the City

On foggy streets tall buildings float;
gravity is nonexistent.
Every apparition that you pass
startles like a person.

A Postcard from Peru

For J.C.

Your postcard flew in today
from Lima, Peru.
I pictured you chewing dried coca leaves
on Machu Picchu –
7000 feet above sea level.

I am with you in the Andes, Joe,
where you are higher
than the ancient Incan ground
you stand on, gazing
at the emerald sky below.

The shadow of a condor
(whose wings span a mountain gorge)
glides across your vision.
The sun kneels among stone ruins;
and the night is history.

In Memoriam

In the flower-filled funeral parlor
my uncle's corpse is on display.
The voices of relatives and friends
sprinkle the parlor with sympathy.
There are old Italian women in black;
always in black, always praying for the repose
of the souls of the dead.
These sorrowful crones seem to live forever.

In his half-open coffin my uncle lies
embalmed and ready for burial.
Looking at him, I remember how much
he enjoyed red wine with his meals.
If only he would belch, as he often did
before his after-dinner nap.

A Painting

For Susan

A bird carries a bit of sky
to the earth when it lands.

Your hands are birds
that spread color.

When you fly winged with vision
into your canvas,

a heartbeat the size
of a flower begins,

and grows till your painting
takes on a life of its own.

Primal Scenes

Janine – love child, now eleven years old –
wherever you are I hope you are loved.
Each new day that you grow beyond my memory,
I discover a truer perspective.
The past seems more real than the present.
Does your cuckoo clock still *cuckoo* the hours?
I remember your mother loved breast-feeding you
while I made gentle love to her.
She said it made her milk sweeter.

At your age, Janine, the innocent eye is blind.
Imagination outshines what you see.
A rose is more than a rose.

Child... daughter, forty-odd years younger,
did your mother and I seem godlike,
when we stood in our nakedness to dress?
I remember the color of your eyes.

Visiting My Parents

When I visit my parents in the country,
A little boy inside me remembers a picnic.
My mother's welcome evokes the scent
Of freshly baked apples on an autumn morning.
In the garden, my father is transplanting
Lombardy poplars. He leans on his shovel
Long enough to shake my hand. My hand
Is a seed growing again in his hand.
The saplings drink-in the light of his presence.
He handles them with fatherly love.

I am the poet-son home from the city,
With its myriad material distractions;
Where all my friends are manic-depressive,
Given to cynicism and promiscuity.
We nourish one another's neuroses.
Why should I burden the lives of my parents
With the trouble I've seen? What do they know
Of a poet's life? I have heard it said –
Life is a comedy to those who think,
And a tragedy to those who feel.

Time past is suspended in time present,
Like a rainbow caught in the spray
Of a waterfall. The slogans of youth
Echo in my memory. Each time I visit
My parents, each visit begins with farewell.
When they grumble about old age, I see
My own mortality reflected in their eyes.

The afternoon lengthens. We lounge
In my father's garden, drinking Chianti.
From a blossoming apple bough, a robin sings.

Grievance

Nowadays there are
too many poets
with degrees;

most of them are
professors
in universities,

moonlighting
as true poets
under the auspices
of approved theses.

In labor union lingo,
they're called scabs.

Il Sangue

For Pier Giorgio Di Cicco

The blood that moves through your language
Moves through mine.
The heart that gives it utterance
Is ours alone.

Come away from that cancer of neon
With its running sores of money.
The city's iron skyline
Bends before the structure of a poem.

Our people work in the Tuscan fields
where the rain walks barefoot,
and the fragrance of the breathing earth
rustles like the body of a woman
reaching out to you in sleep.

Let us play our mandolins and sing
O Sole Mio! The joy is ours.

Strangled by a spaghetti stereotype,
an Italian is supposed to lay bricks.
You build poems with the stars.

Florida

"In God we trust."

Welcome to Florida – the Sunshine State
of perpetual retirement and vitamin C.
The Fountain of Youth sought by Ponce de Leon,
De Soto, and nameless others,
hanging like a fat, flaccid phallus
in the Gulf and Atlantic waters.
Welcome to Florida – from the Latin *floridus*,
meaning flowery – where real estate
is bought and sold by the inch
where even God is trusted, provided he owns
a yacht and plays golf
where orange juice is a mouthwash
where the climate has been translated
into 27 languages
where every day is a legal holiday
where tourism is a necessary social disease
where Canadians hibernate
where cemeteries are kept well-hidden
and death has the smallest neon sign
where the behavior of alligators
and hurricanes is local gossip
where the flora and fauna live next door
to an oceanfront hotel-cum-shopping mall and marina
where money rots on trees
where the Everglades is almost as wild as Miami
where blonde mermaids in green bikinis
train dolphins to act sexy
where the Mafia has a monopoly on swizzle sticks
where Jewish widows buy Jaguars for gigolos
where beauty is truth, if you're beautiful

where everything, including room service, is:
Ideal. Perfect. Excellent.
Please circle one of the above.
Where else can a man compare
the size of his erect penis
to the trunk of a palm tree?
Where else can a woman sun-bathe
beside a kidney-shaped swimming pool
with a frozen daiquiri, suntan oil,
a view of the world's longest beach,
and a squad of gorgeous lifeguards?
Where else can a child remain a child?
Welcome to Florida.
Y'all come back now, y'heah?

Dead Opossums

Driving one night through the "Heart of Dixie,"
the piney woods streaming by me,
I saw a dead opossum on the road...
and then another... and another.
Possum trivia kept me awake at the wheel.
T.S. Eliot's nickname came to mind –
an Algonquian word, meaning *white beast*.
In the early seventeenth century,
Captain John Smith, lover of Pocahontas, wrote:
"An opossum hath a head like a swine,
a taile like a rat, and is of the bignes of a cat."
The male opossum has a forked penis.
When threatened with danger, an opossum
rolls on its side and plays dead.
Y'all know what an Alabama *luau* is?
Roast possum and a six-pack.

Rattlesnake

Riding shotgun with a sideburned stranger
through the flat Texas panhandle,
hungover, wondering what in God's name
I was doing there – nothing but wheatfields,
scrub-covered rangelands for miles around,
my throat parched with dust and too many cigarillos –
suddenly slithered a snake
across the heat-hazy blacktop.
The stranger swerved his pickup truck to hit it... missed...
we skidded screeching to a stop.

We found the snake, a prairie rattler,
coiled, rattling, in a clump of grass.
The stranger blew off its wedge-shaped head
with one blast from his handgun.
Grinning a good-ol'-boy, Texas-bred, kick-ass grin,
he dangled his trophy in the air.
Ever eat snake? he said. His jackknife flashed.

The six-button rattle felt brittle, light as a pinecone.
I kept it for good luck.
The wind in the grasses hissed.
I was a thousand miles from home.

Untitled

My friend and I sat in a gloomy roadhouse
outside Lexington, Kentucky,
drinking draft beer and not saying much.
Our overheated Chevy sat in Vern's Radiator Shop.
"If it heats or if it leaks call Vern."
A skinny little boy of five or six, in need of a bath,
was amusing himself with the jukebox and pinball machine.
His parents were drinking. It was midafternoon.
The boy grew restless and whiny,
and, tired of eating potato chips,
began pressing his mother for attention.
The father was only a smell.
Grabbing her child and shaking him,
the mother snarled: *Hush! You wanna go home?*

Picnic on Chickamauga Battlefield

It is a June afternoon in rural Georgia.
In the shade of an ancient white oak
a woman and I are picnicking
on Chickamauga battlefield.

Monuments, field guns, cannonball markers
clash with picnic tables, shady lovers' lanes...
"My great-granddaddy died here," the woman says,
"fighting for the Confederacy."

Sightseers stroll by. I think of that scene
in *Gone With the Wind* – the burning of Atlanta –
and softly whistle "Dixie."
What I know of the War Between the States

is reflected in the woman's gray eyes –
a grassy, creek-winding, rolling woodland
through which death once raged.
And it seems death is still out of breath.

Robinson Jeffers

To contain his double-axed rage, he built by hand
a stone tower on the California coast.
The tower was his refuge from humankind.
He preferred the company of hawks and rocks,
wrote passionate poems in praise of them.
"I'd sooner, except the penalties, kill a man than a hawk."
By giving his "inhumanism" a god's utterance,
he made it sound like the noblest of virtues.
Although he apologized for his bad dreams,
it was with the knowledge that evil is only human.

Tennessee Williams, 1977

In his hotel room on the U. of Notre Dame campus
sat Tennessee Williams. With him
were two young men lying half-naked in bed,
like Siamese twins on an operating table.
It was a strange scene, almost stagey.
Earlier that evening, in Washington Hall,
Mr. Williams brought down the house
when he toasted *Our Lady* in his best Southern drawl.
Now looking sweetly fatigued from his one-night stand,
he offered me wine. I drank to his health,
to the living theatre of the man.
I told him he looked more Italian than I.
"It must be osmosis," he said.
I didn't know whether to act straight or hip;
but I went away wishing
I'd kissed his hand instead of shaking it.

The Brig

U.S. Naval Receiving Station, Brooklyn, N.Y.

It wasn't his three months' confinement
but the humiliating absurdity
of scrubbing the latrine with a toothbrush
that made the prisoner crack.

We were singing hymns in the officers' mess
that served for a chapel on Sundays.
Out the high barred windows
the morning sky was iron-colored.

His mind was fragile as the waterglass
he wrapped in a dishtowel to deaden
the noise when he smashed it
and tried to swallow the shards.

We could not see his face for the blood,
did not want to see the despair
and horror that reflected our own,
as two Marine guards dragged him away.

The Death of Robert Desnos

When night came to Buchenwald
with glaring searchlights and wolflike dogs,
the poet looked for a hole
in the sky. It was not the moon
that he saw among black clouds
but his own skull wreathed with barbed wire.

382-44-9842

The silence echoes the steel celldoors
slamming shut.

What is more impersonal
than a hard-on in prison?

My lust for the pinup girl died
quivering in my hand
under a gray woolen blanket
in cellblock eleven.

A Girl on the Subway

Not just a girl, but one in denim shorts
with a red heart-shaped patch that shouted:
Help! I Need Lovin!

There she sat, a book in her lap,
wearing her mood like a charm bracelet,
while the subway train thundered
into each station.

She looked sixteen going on thirty;
as if she sat waiting for where she was
to catch up with where she was at.

Below advertisements that promised
clear skin, *free delivery*, *sex for life*,
she crossed her long bare legs
and opened her book.

Nymphet, tart, Lolita. Says who?
'Twas the book's title caught my eye:
No Language But a Cry.

Woman in Labor

For her sweet sake, the world should be
A streamlined womb with chrome-plated parts.

In the maternity ward, I visualize births regular as cars
Rolling off an assembly line.

Entering her room, I see her magnified with life
In a sterile bed – thirsty, travailing.

It hurts like hell, she whimpers.
Unable to help, I feel conspicuously useless.
My presence becomes a labor of waiting.

The Abortion

With a do-it-yourself abortion kit,
she prepared herself for a little death.
Fear and a grim resolve attended her.
She was two months pregnant.

First, she boiled a watery solution
of sodium chloride;
next she sterilized a syringe;
and then she began squirting the solution
into her cervix.

She tried to relax
till sharp cramps came
(worse than menstrual)
and some dark blood clotted with pieces of tissue,
and more blood...
She was sweating pain.

To the bathroom she staggered –
pale, nauseated, dry-mouthed,
feeling as though her uterus
had been yanked inside out.

Still Life

Imagine a white oilcloth-covered table,
and on it a glass of red wine, bread, a dish
of black olives, and some Gorgonzola cheese.
Now imagine my octogenarian grandfather
ringing a handball as he pushes his handcart
along the tree-lined streets of his neighborhood,
sharpening people's knives. Imagine him
returning home at noon to this still life,
and partaking of it with the gusto of an artist.

Tourists

Conspicuous as flags
on a windy day.

Always in groups or pairs
hogging the foreground, sharing
a tableau, focusing cameras,
cracking guidebooks, peeling maps
chewing timetables…

They need something to look at
that won't look back –
a monument, a view
with a room around it.

To a Young Actress Out of Work in Montreal

To B.M.

There isn't enough work for an actress in Montreal,
I've heard you complaining time and again.
And you are tired of bilingual theatre
With its double-tongued politics;
Tired of playing Mother Goose
Pour les enfants de la bourgeoisie
Who prefer Batman to Little Bo-Peep;
So tired of being out of work that, instead of sheep,
You count curtain calls till you fall asleep.
How will you cruise control your career?
The choices are obstacle courses, my dear.
Hitchhike to Hollywood and discover yourself.
Land a speaking part in a low-budget skin flick.
Move to Toronto – home of the homesick.
Find a sugar daddy. Go on welfare –
Tell 'em you're supporting a habit: you like to eat.
After all, *the world's a stage*.
I have seen you on rue Ste. Catharine in freezing March,
With your feathered boa and silver Wedgies,
Upstaging the gay libbers.
You could revamp Vivien Leigh's Blanche DuBois
And ride another streetcar – one that loops
Around desire and oblivion.
I know the stage transforms you,
And you are most alive as someone else.
I have heard you speaking the speech "trippingly on the
        tongue";
Watched you suiting "the action to the word."

Airy as a ballerina,
You don't even cast a shadow.
For those of us, like you, who can't make it
In the straight world – life's a bummer.
Pity the dreamers. Their dreams are crowded
With a raging loneliness.

My heart auditions for you.
I hope you find work soon.

Elegy

Port Hope: A 52-year-old woman who disappeared from her home on Sept. 22, was found dead in a tree. Police say the woman was found fully-clothed in a sitting position up a tree near the lakefront. The body went unnoticed until all the leaves fell off.

The Toronto Sun, November 13, 1975

Perhaps she had a covenant with nature,
or a death wish that coincided
with the autumnal equinox
of her disappearance. Who knows?
That she chose a tree to die in was peculiar,
as though some primal force in her took root.
But what kind of tree did that woman choose?
How did she climb it?
A druid tree whose leafy branches
almost touched the ground...
And what did the birds do when they saw her body
perched in a tree day after day?
Did they flock to her like a nest?
Did they sing? Or was their singing
silenced by her silence?
Did squirrels bury seeds and nuts
in her pockets?

During the long Ontario autumn nights
she shrank into herself –
a stiff, dry branch
stuck in the wind's throat.
The autumn leaves prepared her shroud.
Along the lakefront her colors were scattered.

When all the leaves fell,
the skeletal tree became her catafalque
in which she sat fully-clothed –
a scarecrow uprooted;
a fugitive from Gothic romance;
a phantom Daphne embraced by branches.

If suicide is a spurious valor,
to die alone in a tree
transcends all knowledge of good and evil.
And what of the tree, with its knot of darkness?
A tree is a tree…
How that beautifully mad, middle-aged dryad
truncated her family tree
is a subject for poets as well as police.

Let the strange circumstances of that woman's death
blossom in the hearts of those who would bury her.
The tree's roots have already dug her grave.

Tekahionwake

I would rather have come by canoe
than by car to Chiefswood,
singing *The Song My Paddle Sings*;

but this is another age,
and her ancestral mansion
on the north bank of the Grand River

is now an Ontario museum
filled with period furniture
and Indian artifacts.

In one of its roped-off rooms
I pocketed a string of shell beads,
and exulted in my theft.

O Tekahionwake, may your spirit
forgive me. Around my neck
I wear your wampum like an amulet.

In grade school, I learned
some of your verses by heart.
The Train Dogs was my favorite:

Out of the night and the north;
Savage of breed and of bone,
Shaggy and swift comes the yelping band...

You were a true Mohawk princess.
To commemorate you, Canada split your persona
on a five-cent postage stamp.

I see you in buckskin garb,
an eagle feather in your hair,
giving a recital for the Indians' sake.

How many war-painted braves
would have broken their arrows
just to hear you singing?

Mako Sica

Myriads of stars glittered –
the August night we bedded down
in the South Dakota badlands.
Wind-bitten sandstone buttes
and deep, dry gullies
carved a silence so pure
we could hear the wind dragging
a coyote's yawn through the sagebrush.

In that barren landscape
the Sioux stampeded buffalo over cliffs,
and praised the deathly thunder.
White settlers knew fears worse than hunger
as they rolled westward in covered wagons,
cursing their dreams.

We lay awake in our sleeping bags,
within reach of roadmap and car,
feeling some nameless fear
creep into the stillness –
a fear as old as the starlit fossils
exhumed by the erosion around us.

Lines Written After a Sleepless Night

As I grow older
the future creeps nearer,
lengthening the past.
I am the same age
my father was
when I was AWOL from the USN.

In this subtropical seaport,
the humidity hangs
thick as Spanish moss.
Cicadas sting the air with song.
My thoughts breed
a dark morning.

Consider the serpent
that crawls out of its skin
several times a year,
and the religions
we burden ourselves with
to become holy.

On the Eve of My Thirty-Sixth Birthday

Sometimes the night exists for me alone.
Sinking into an opium sleep that turns
Me slowly inside out, my body burns
Like that legendary bird on its throne
Of ashes. When I cast the second stone,
It bounces back at me. My heart unlearns
Its metaphors, and comes to newer terms
With mortality. Now would I atone
For everything but love on my birthday
(If I could), singing of the imaged word
Till death, broken-winged in a bright meadow,
Echoes each feathery note back to clay.
And so I am; and sometimes like that bird
I stand in the grave of my own shadow.

Most People Don't Want to Be Told

Most people don't want to be told
about suffering and evil;
about the Crusades, the Inquisition, the Holocaust;
that over one fifth of the world's population
lives on less than a dollar a day...
Most people say: *What has that got to do with me?*
I wouldn't hurt a fly. I pay my taxes.
God helps those who help... et cetera.
Most people don't want to be told about death.
Most people don't want to be told about life.
What most people want
is not to have to think for themselves.
Dante's vision of hell pales beside
Christianity's hellish history on earth.

After Reading Dostoevsky's *Notes from Underground*

For Ed Bruski, wherever he is

Sometimes I too feel like a character
in a nineteenth-century Russian novel:
one of those morose, solitary creatures
given to boredom and low debauchery,
for whom life is as meaningless and grim
as this planet that revolves in its doom-
starred course, like a bomb through space.
Then I consider the unreal but egotistic
roles we play to survive among our kind;
and in the consciousness of my despair
know that twice two will always equal four,
because everything is a necessary lie.

The Night After Christmas

In the blue candlelight
of this late hour,
when the caroling is over
and the cease-fire broken,

I stare out the window
and wonder what power
will grant this warring world
its wish for extinction.

Poinsettia

Outside the window of my room
December snow lights up the darkness.
Tchiakovsky's *First Symphony* is playing
On the clock radio.

In its plastic pot a poinsettia glows.
Each whorl of bright red bracts
Surrounds a tiny flower cluster
And fans out into space – to the very edge

Of that space the lower leaves
Fill with green shadows.
From the strain of so much self-illumination
The poinsettia's fragrance is exhausted.

The Snow Woman

Naked, she looks at herself
in a full-length mirror.
Her smile freezes.

To Mary Jane, On Her Twenty-Ninth Birthday

The full moon through the elm
follows your shadow
as you walk in a black dress that breathes.

The March night air your heat
perfumes. Ah, never was a kiss
so created like a poem.

May the universe dance
to the rhythm of your womb,
your womb which is a grave and a garden.

May love intensify
the bliss of your senses.
Now take your own hand and be what you have become.

Under the Ambassador Bridge

I sat on a park bench
under the Ambassador Bridge,
watching people make pests of the gulls.

Across the river, in Detroit,
the sun was melting behind a steel mill.
The river smelled of algae, oil, sludge...

From a concrete pier
a straw-hatted black man was fishing.
Not even the shadows of fishes were biting.

Sunk to its gunwales, a tugboat
towing a rust-caked barge chugged by.
A bell buoy clanged.

The western sky glowed acid red.
The bridge hovered over me.
A white feather blew along the riverbank.

Wyoming

1

As I climbed out of Shell Canyon
in the Bighorn Mountains,
I saw the shades of Shoshone braves
carrying armfuls of moonlight on horseback.

2

At an empty roadside rest area
I stopped the car to stretch my legs
and came upon an antlered elk drinking
the summer moonlight from a mountain stream
that sang in its stony bed.

A dry wind blew westerly.
Solitude, wilderness, Wyoming surrounded me.
For the longest moment I thought of ditching the car
and finding my way back on foot
to the natural order of things.

Montana

"Big sky" country.
In a town of few words
a few mangy-looking locals
in cowboy boots
sit in the town's only cafe
trying hard not to stare at us
as we drink our coffee.
Thumb-tacked to the wall
behind an antique cash register
a bold-faced poster says –
The only reason some people are alive
is because it's against the law to kill them.

Only in America

On hearing the news
of Elvis Presley's death,
a Hollywood press agent remarked:
"Good career move."

Prison Yard

High prison walls crowned with razor wire
Give a stark perspective of the sky,
As if the sky might suddenly fall.
So magnified is the midmorning sky,

You can see it with your eyes shut.
The light is bright, the light is bright and hard.
In the high-walled, guard-towered prison yard
Ten prisoners are playing basketball

On a concrete court. How vigorously
They run… jump… yell… dribble the ball.
Alone or in groups, smoking cigarettes,
The lifers dawdle, old beyond recall.

The guards blink through their boredom at the yard.
One burly guard is shaking down a black.
What are you in for? croaks a jailbird.
Someone snorts: *Money don't love you back.*

On a wooden bench you sit, killing time
Killing time, with your back to the wall,
Watching the dead wall's shadow harden,
And wishing the goddamned sky would fall.

Night Train

Mile on mile the train rumbles westward
through the empty Saskatchewan night.
The hour is late. The passengers are asleep.
I put away the book I've been reading
and imagine myself as someone else.
Across the aisle from me
a bottle blonde in tiger leotards
sits with her sleeping child.
I know her life story.
By the time we reach our destinations,
she will have told me mine.

Rejection Slip

Our poetry backlog
is sequoia-like in bulk.
We are not even accepting
laurel leaves.

344 Davenport Road

1
After a yearlong absence
in which I did nothing
but read, write, and loaf,
I returned alone to Toronto –
the city of dreadful day –
eager to renew my fantastic neuroses
and the life-style it took to perfect them.

In August, the year Elvis died,
I subleased a bright studio
on Davenport Road
from a German masseuse
I met at a party.
(She was flying to Shangri-La
with her sugar daddy.)
We were lovers a very short time.

With my typewriter, and clothes,
and boxes of books,
I moved into the studio
on Davenport Road,
and phoned every woman I knew,
including my ex-wife who threatened
to sue me for nonsupport
if I continued to live "like a gypsy."
Well, I lived as I did
in order to write poems –
"the most fatiguing of occupations,"
an American poet once said.

I moved around a lot
because staying in one place
reminded me that where I belonged
no longer existed.

2
In my studio, the skylight
fixed its Cyclops eye on me
and on the *Sleeping Nude* of Modigliani.
My back door opened onto a fire escape
that glowed with potted geraniums.

Most days I sweated words,
literally drenching myself
in their colors and sounds,
trying to make them sing.

Monogamous with my Muse,
I was 36, the autumn of youth;
highly sexed, on a lyric quest
for objective experience.

My studio became a stopover
for friends with vague destinations
and vaguer itineraries.
(New Orleans is the only city in North America
that has streets named after the nine Muses.)

3

On Halloween, I saw my two children
for the first time in three years.
They had grown quite tall,
and the masks they wore were their faces.
I wondered if the past
had changed more than the present.

4

The winter solstice augured well and ill.
I met a lady lawyer,
full beautiful – an Aries child;
her hair was blonde, her legs were long…
We fell in love,
and that was our downfall.

5

The Roman poet Sextus Propertius wrote:
Non datur ad Musas currere lata via.
There is no royal road to poetry.

To My Father

Having argued with you, confided in you,
and sometimes listened to you
for most of my thirty-six years
on this accidental planet,
I think it's time we had a man-to-man talk.

I confess I'm selfish and willful –
perhaps hereditarily so.
I won't make excuses. You told me long ago
if I took my troubles to the market,
I'd come back with my own.

Well, father, avid birdwatcher that you are –
the blasted oak in which you placed a birdhouse
still puts forth leaves. Did it sprout
from an acorn a bluejay forgot?
Is life a half-remembered dream?

The only difference is, your dreams
are more practical than mine.
You point out the poison mushrooms, then rave about
their elfin beauty. You add; I subtract.
I am your prodigal freedom enslaved by memory.

When you were burdened with worry
and an aching back, you boarded a train
for Buffalo, New York, and journeyed all night
just to visit me in jail.
A fellow jailbird said: "That's what I call a father!"

In my deepest shame, I felt proud to be your son.
I remember when you spared the rod.
You made me read
The Complete Lectures of Robert G. Ingersoll.
That book spoiled my belief in God.

Although our philosophies sometimes clash,
we try to respect each other's space.
The craft I've taken so long to learn
reveals its lines upon your face.
Wisdom reads the heart; age has that advantage.

The Old Barn

The old barn sits in a field
of weeds and brambles.
It clings to the landscape like a rampike.
Emptied of everything but cobwebs, mice,
and the twittering, fork-tailed swallows that nest
under its rain-sunken roof
the old barn is a lost landmark.
The seasons stumble over it,
and trespass on the cropless acres
it once commanded.

Winter Solstice

It took the snow all day
To bury the shadow
Of a white birch tree.

Lyric

Softly she wakens
from the dark seed of her sleep.

The sunlight
sits on our bed like a cat licking butter.

When her hand touches me,
my skinechoes the sound

a hummingbird makes
in the throat of a flower.

When I whisper her name,
a leaf holds its breath
till it falls.

Nocturne

The crickets stridulate.
With spools of black thread
they sew the shadows together.

Homage to Walter Anderson

To paint an octopus dying in the arms
of its own iridescence
was Walter Anderson's way of looking
into the eye of God.

Guided by pelicans,
he sailed his green skiff to Horn Island,
and made "a progress"
painting its flora and fauna.

To study the sequence of color,
he painted a stranded Portuguese man-of-war
whose gas-filled lung convulsively glowed
each time a wave washed over it.

Oh that we too might see the purpleness
inside a dried mangrove root
when the wood is broken,
and dance for one endless moment
with a vision numinous and natural.

On First Looking into *The Horn Island Logs of Walter Inglis Anderson*

Much have I traveled in the natural world,
and many natural wonders seen;
round many campfires have I sat
listening to the music of trees,
as the wind plucked different chords from each;
yet I never saw nature objectively
till I read Anderson's *Horn Island Logs*,
and realized nature is its own metaphor.

In the beginning was the image.
The imaged word I found
by going to the forest, to the cactus desert,
to any uncultivated tract of land
and observing how wildflowers
are pushed up by creation's hand.

The imaged word was a boat-tailed grackle
preening his iridescent black plumage
in a Mississippi saltmarsh at sunrise.
It was a bull moose with antlers the size of a rocking chair.
A fledgling jay unseen yet heard
launching its alarmed cry from an oak bough
arched above a stream of traffic.
It was the green death mask of kudzu.
A sunny pond blooming with spatterdock.
Orange lichens eating into a weathered rock...

Seeing ripened my eyes. The images I saw
ripened within. With my eyes closed
I could smell the difference
between a white rose and a red rose.

Birdwatching

Birds are holes in heaven through which man may pass.
Walter Anderson

In the nursing home, I guide my father
enfeebled by Alzheimer's to a large window
looking out on a thickety ravine.
His arms hang down numbly,
as he shuffles pajamaed and slippered
past invalids dozing in wheelchairs.
Outside, the spring air pulses with birds.
A bluejay lights on a birch tree, and preens itself.
Twice I call his attention to it.
His face is expressionless.
The jay flies away. He stands there.

My father once knew his birds like a book,
reveled in their colors and songs.
Now he's on the other side of time.
He's forgotten everything, even death.
The nurse says he eats well and chuckles a lot.
I want to shout: *Look, dad – a purple martin!*
a red-tailed hawk! and see his delight.
I want to carry his binoculars,
and birdwatch with him all morning
by some shady woodland pool.

Confused and memoryless, my father
stares out the window.
There are birds in his eyes;
but his mind doesn't see them.

Out of Time

For Donna

All summer long I've lived on Pacific time.
Your absence has thrown my timing off.
Whenever I glance at a clock
I wonder what you have already done
Or you will be doing on Eastern time.
Sometimes we phone each other
And forget whose time we're on.
Ours is a past-future relationship.
Do I think of you before or after you think of me?
I think love is a spatiotemporal phenomenon
That has frequent fits of relativity.

I'm tired of tides, sunsets, and once upon a time.
I'm tired of borrowed time and daylight saving time.
I'm tired of Father Time and auld lang syne.
I'm tired of losing time, finding time,
Keeping time, wasting time, killing time...
No matter which time zone,
I am tired of time all the time.
When I return to you,
We shall kiss till we turn to stone.

Vancouver, B.C., 1986

To a Friend

You, the white sheep of your Mafia family,
with grizzled beard, hands like a cardplayer's,
and clipped New York City accent,
still consult the *I Ching* before breakfast,
wondering if chance is synchronous with fate.
Under your sign Dante Alighieri died.
By his own spirit he was deified.
Dear Jungian friend, do you still believe
a dream is the mind's distorting mirror
in which one's shadow is reflected?
Unlike your shrewd old gangster father
whom you seldom saw or understood,
you never married your heaven to your hell
nor your evil to your good.

Baudelaire's Sketch of Jeanne Duval

How is it that her animal allure
distorts my reason, makes me brood over trivia.
What strange sorcery does she practise,
that my soul succumbs to pure desire
and seeks in her the eternal feminine?

At night I sit, laudanum brandy in hand,
watching her dance a voodoo love dance.
Such wealth of buttocks, breasts that defy
gravity, lips you could trip over.
The musk she sweats is my fetish.

And why is it always always, always
the eleventh minute after every hour?
Une succube vit dans ma Venus noire.
Tired but unsated, she fevers my sleep
with her lust. My soul she devours.

Transvestite

Because he was born with the wrong body,
his clothing is a bruise that will not heal.
Posing before a mirror in his room,
he transmogrifies his sex with lingerie,
and turns over another leaf
to reveal a different fig.
Untroubled by the spotty bleeding
of his anus, it behooves him
to make a pageant of his pain.
If it wasn't for the sanitary pad
he wears like a woman,
he would almost feel pregnant.

Unholy Sonnet

December dark and snowy ends the year –
Year of the Dragon – 1988 –
The year of my obsession with Baudelaire,
Whose poetry and syphilitic fate
Demonized the Muses forevermore.
All year I saw cockroaches in my sleep;
I dreamed dreams that I never dreamed before.
Now the Christmasy glitter of Bloor Street
Carols me churchward to Christmas Eve Mass,
Where I recapture my childhood at will.
All is calm, all is bright. All flesh is grass.
Over the creche hovers Calvary hill.
Is it myrrh I smell, or the Devil's breath?
The virgin-whore has given birth to death.

Chthonic Light

For Leslie Thompson

"Driven by demonic, chthonic powers,"
I delve into my unconscious.
In the light you celebrate, I see the darkness
that surrounds a rotting nurselog
whose hollows of tangled hemlock roots
are graves aswarm with moss.
When you focus your camera lens to form an image,
tendrils of fog appear, light is reflected
in a blur of rain-forest ferns…
the Earth Spirit wakens,
groping in roots, tapering in tree trunks,
with the energy of a serpent.

Epigram

This is the forest primeval;
And still it is to MacMillan Bloedel –
A tree parasite capable
Of dooming the earth to a treeless hell.

Where Does the Marbled Murrelet Nest?

The nesting habitat of the marbled murrelet remains unsolved, and presents an intriguing problem to ornithologists.

The Audubon Nature Encyclopedia

Out of the misty northwest night
From the darkening surge of the sea,
The marbled murrelet inland flies.
Its nesting place is a mystery.

All day the murrelet dives for fish.
At dusk, they gather in rafts offshore;
Then disappear into the darkness
Till they flock to the sea once more.

Where does the marbled murrelet nest?
In trees, on cliffs, or in burrows?
Wherever it nests is a secret
That only the marbled murrelet knows.

Parts of a Flower

For Leslie Thompson

A flower will do anything
to get pollinated.
It makes no secret of its secret.
I want to plant kisses all over your body,
so more kisses will grow
and you will always feel kissed.

Poem

The meaning of flowering
is that the speck of protoplasm
inside the pollen grain
which is in the anther
which is borne on the stamen
which is enclosed by the petals
shall find its way
to the bit of protoplasm
which is within the ovule
which is in the ovary
which is inside the pistil
at the heart of the flower

Skyscape

After a thunderstorm, the wide prairie sky
Waits for the sun to hang out white clouds to dry.

In a Country Churchyard

I must borrow from Archibald Lampman
to praise this midsummer afternoon
in a country churchyard on Highway 3,
several farmhouses east of Morpeth, Ontario.

I know by heart the words on Lampman's cairn —
some fragment of a sonnet, its mood
and outlook so undaunted, so sublime,
so existentially at odds with mine…

I saunter past the steepled, redbrick
Anglican church (erected 1845)
and sit among weathered gravestones
in the spruce-scented shade, half in love

with death, yet loath to despair,
scornful of hope and its sanguine *sursum corda,*
per aspera ad astra chorus, knowing
(as I listen to a sparrow singing,

lie on the grass and look at white clouds,
have an erotic daydream, consider my resources…)
life is either a deadly and unknown law,
or a business which doesn't cover expenses.

Ah, welladay! Yonder south Lake Erie
flashes. A fly buzzes about my head.
The churchyard breathes the scent of evergreens,
and the late afternoon light is golden.

At 37, Archibald Lampman died –
perhaps knowing he was most alive
buried deepest in the work he loved,
perhaps knowing he had glimpsed eternity.

September 22, 1990

On a treeless roadside
ragged with litter,
the sun has sewn
bright yellow buttons of tansies.

Rain

Pacific Rim National Park, British Columbia

In the rain forest, rain is regnant,
rain sets the theme, dripping
off leaves and branches, trickling
down trunks, flowing among mosses,
liverworts, lichens, ferns… soaking
into the florest floor.
There is rain
on the cloud-topped Douglas firs,
rain on the red cedars
with their thin stringy bark,
rain on the hemlocks
encrusted with lichens,
rain on our faces, our sylvan faces,
rain on our hands which are bare.
There is rain
on a green gloomy solitude.
The sound of the ocean is unheard;
but a mountain stream gives rhythm to the rain.
We are sinking into the atmosphere
of the rain forest. Our faces
are wet with the rain.
We appear to each other out of bark.
Everything in us is scented,
like a balsam fir.
Green is the rain; green is the beauty
born of the rain.

Moment

The child looks at the ball.
The ball wants to play.

Toy Trucks

For Lowell

He likes to play with his toy trucks
    And make his evening rounds.
He drives his trucks from room to room,
    Uttering trucklike sounds.

The red fire-engine enchants him,
    With ladders, hose, and bell.
The other trucks are traffic-jammed,
    Forgotten for a spell.

A dump truck chips an earthen vase.
    He nods his drowsy head.
His father puts the trucks away
    And steers him straight to bed

Prelude to a Life

This is my earliest childhood memory.
One rainy night I refused to go to bed
unless my mother let me throw our pet cat
out of my upstairs bedroom window.
She handed me the cat.

For several days it limped around our house, avoiding me.
I am haunted by this memory,
humbled by the hard knowledge
that no crime is complete until it's confessed,
because conscience is the will to be guilty.

In My Father's Garden

To stand in my father's garden
fragrant after a spring rain
and feel the wet earth under my bare feet
is a soul massage so sensuously deep
that I know how a flower must feel
when it puts forth a blossom.

1
It's raining on the garden –
on clover, broom, bouncing Bet...
It's raining seeds of water.
Every plant is blooming wet.

2
Over a red honeysuckle
the hummingbird hovers –
a winged jewel and its setting
reflecting each other.

3
Along a weathered wood fence
tall hollyhocks stand at attention,
emblazoned with blossoms whose colors
only a rainbow parades.

4

Under an old crab-apple tree
where ants have built their nest
stands a yellow-shafted flicker
eating the ants with zest.

5

The garden spider spins its web,
spins it thread by silken thread
till the thread stretched strong and tight
can stop a katydid in flight.

6

In the insect-humming heat
of a summer afternoon,
a toad squats under a rhubarb leaf,
waiting for evening.

7

On summer nights when crickets sing,
and the air is so still it's listening,
in slow wavy flight fireflies flash
signals to attract their mates in the grass.

8

Bald cypress trees stand
leafless and gaunt,
dripping with moss,
knee-deep in a swamp.

9

The anole inhabits trees and shrubs,
and feeds on spiders, insects, grubs.
It changes the color of its scaly skin
to brown or green by the mood it's in.

10

It is a hazy August afternoon.
A cicada chirrs. No songbird sings.
The only breeze in the garden is
a white butterfly fluttering its wings.

11

Birch-yellow, oak-brown, maple-red.
The autumn woods are stained
with the colors of birds
that in them sang and nested.

12

Under a bare elm
stands a solitary crow
silhouetted
against the whiteness of a garden
after the first night of snow.

The Earthworm

To observe the common earthworm
Going about its earthy chores
Requires a fisherman's patience
Because it seldom goes outdoors.

This wriggly pink invertebrate
Has no eyes, no ears, nose, nor chin;
But no matter, it has five hearts,
And breathes through its sensitive skin.

The worm digs underground all day,
And comes out in the dewy night
To eat dead leaves, or seek a mate –
Another moist hermaphrodite.

Garter Snake

In the tall grass around my tent,
A snake's tongue licked the air for scent.

Winding its way along the ground,
The snake appeared without a sound.

Dark-brown it was, and yellow-striped:
A harmless garter. Down I swooped

On it. It curled, it lashed its tail,
It tried to bite my fingernail.

There was a strange and pungent smell.
My hands felt wet; the snake as well.

The frightened serpent had the sense
To discharge musk in self-defense.

If only for your nose's sake,
Do not pick up a garter snake.

Mockingbird

In Audubon Park, early one day,
I heard the raucous call of a jay.

Then a red robin's ringing song
Hurried the spring morning along.

A titmouse whistled. *Caw*, cried a crow.
Chirrup, cheree, preached a vireo.

From high up in a sycamore tree
Came the woodnote of a wood pewee.

Suddenly a mockingbird I saw,
Whose singing was a grand opera.

Of all the songs that day I heard,
None compared with the mockingbird's.

Chickadees

For Jill

On winter mornings the chickadees flock
    To the tree outside my window,
And pry under the bark for insect eggs
    Among the branches high and low.

Chick-a-dee-dee-dee, they whistle their name
    And hop about like acrobats.
In wintry weather they flock together,
    Wearing shiny black scarves and caps.

The Butcher-Bird

The butcher-bird, or northern shrike,
    Whose song is but a cry,
Spears a leopard frog on a thorn,
    And leaves it there to die.

The butcher-bird is robin-sized
    But has a hawk-like bill.
When he perches on a fencepost,
    Small birds keep deathly still.

He surveys the open woodland,
    Then very butcher-like,
Flies to a nearby locust tree
    And picks the bones of mice.

Alphabet Birds

A is for Anhinga
That swims like a snake

B is for Bittern
That stands very straight

C is for Cuckoo
Whose nest is untidy

D is for Duck
Quacking, waddling and diving

E is for Eagle
Golden or bald

F is for Flamingo
Legs, neck and all

G is for Gull
Gliding over the bay

H is for Hummingbird
Sipping nectar all day

I is for Ibis
That fishes with its bill

J is for Junco
That nests on the ground

K is for Kingfisher
Shaggy of crest

L is for Loon
Yodeling at dusk

M is for Magpie
Whose green tail is long

N is for Nuthatch
Often seen upside down

O is for Owl
Whose shadow has eyes

P is for Pelican
With a pouch half its size

Q is for Quetzal
Tropically feathered

R is for Robin
That likes rainy weather

S is for Swan
On a river afloat

T is for Tanager
Atop an old oak

U is for Umbrella bird
Wearing a headdress

V is for Vulture
That eats… can you guess?

W is for Woodpecker
Pecking holes in a tree

X is for Xenops
Whose song is a squeak

Y is for Yellowlegs
Once hunted for game

Z is for Zebra finch
That is kept in a cage

Have You Ever Seen a Slimy Gray Slug?

Have you ever seen
A slimy gray slug?
It isn't half worm
Nor is it half bug,
But resembles a snail
Minus the shell.

The slimy gray slug
Has a toothlike tongue
And a foot for a belly.
It drags the tide
Inland with the slime
From its body.

Fiddler Crab

When the tide has ebbed
and the sun is low,
a fiddler crab climbs cautiously
out of his muddy burrow
in a mangrove swamp,
waves his large blue claw at a female,
and dances, dances, dances.

Snapping Turtle

A snapping turtle with mud-covered carapace
clambers out of the pond's weedy shallows
and thrusts its ancient, stonelike head
through the bulrushes.

Under the dome of its shell
it pauses to rest...
then lumbers on, dragging
its long sawtooth tail over the wet grass,

across a dirt road, to the edge
of a cornfield, where it digs a hole
with its clawed hind feet,
and lays round white eggs in the rainy dawn.

I Once Had a Pet Praying Mantis

I once had a pet praying mantis
    That perched on a plant in my room.
His name, by the way, was Goliath.
    I fed him dead flies with a spoon.

Goliath was leaf-green in color,
    And long as Pinocchio's nose.
Although he moved awkwardly on foot,
    On instinct he knew how to pose,

With spiny forelegs upraised in prayer –
    Ready, like the jaws of a trap,
To clamp shut over hard-shelled beetles
    Or caterpillars growing fat.

My pet's table manners were horrid.
    Whether it was daytime or night,
He ate more than his weight in insects
    And more than his great appetite.

I took Goliath outdoors one day
    And left him in a flower-bed.
With large bulging eyes he stared at me,
    Then turned his triangular head.

Now guess what happened to Goliath?
    Under a tall bright buttercup
The female mantis he was courting
    Bit off his head, then ate him up.

Lines to a Ladybug

The ladybug is a dainty beetle
    With polka-dotted wings,
And a welcome sight to gardeners
    For the good luck she brings.
Look! the ladybug lightly walks
Upside down on a long leafstalk.
Away she flies – a scarlet speck
That rids most plants of insect pests.
Unlike the ant, she doesn't take
The honeydew that aphids make;
But in fruit trees and flowerbeds
Simply eats the aphids instead.

The Bombardier Beetle

Of the bombardier beetle beware.
It makes use of chemical warfare,
    And lives up to its name
    By taking straight aim
At a hungry toad's goggle-eyed stare.

Walkingstick

The spindle-legged walkingstick
    Looks like what it isn't.
Standing motionless on a twig,
    It looks more twig than insect.

The walkingstick is nature's trick
    Of camouflaged survival.
The hungry bird that preys on it
    Will hardly get a mouthful.

Less agile than the grasshopper
    To which it is related,
The walkingstick can lose a leg
    And then regenerate it.

The Thingumajig

For Lowell

Of all the things that go bump in the night,
The most bumptious is the thingumajig.
It may not give you a shuddering fright,
But – *ouch!* it can pinch like an earwig.

If I Were a Dragonfly

If I were a dragonfly,
    I would hover and skim
Over a white-lilied pond
    Where black whirligigs swim.

On a cattail I would rest,
    With gauzy wings outspread;
Dart after a mosquito
    As it hums overhead.

Like my ancestors that lived
    Millions of years ago –
Those giant *Meganeura*
    Found fossilized in coal,

I too would live on the wing
    Under blue summer skies –
The devil's darning needle,
    With a face full of eyes.

A Lesson in Taxonomy

If you're troubled by taxonomy,
    There's no need to make a fuss.
Just remember that the bumblebee
    Is *Bombus americanus*.

The first name refers to the genus;
    The second specifies its type.
Is there a scientific lesson
    Hidden in all this Latin hype?

Yellow loosestrife sounds more flowerlike
    Than *Lysimachia terrestris*.
Would it be rude to call the robin
    A *Turdus migratorius*?

You can thank a Swedish botanist
    For thinking up this system.
His name was Carl von Linne – also known as
    Linnaeus, Carolus.

The Centipede

You seldom see the centipede.
When you do, it's unexpected.
It moves with such amazing speed,
All its legs seem disconnected.

The centipede lives under rocks
And in the cellar of your house.
With its scurrying legs it looks
So much scarier than a mouse.

It has a pair of poison fangs
That can inflict a painful bite.
So beware. The many-legged centipede
Always hunts at night.

Tree of Heaven

Ailanthus altissima

This tall weed-tree looks tropical,
    And grows where trees grow not.
Its fernlike leaves make a jungle
    Of a vacant city lot.

It grows around old factories
    And in older neighborhoods,
And prefers backyards and alleys
    To shady parks and woods.

Heavenward climbs this hardy tree
    Whose crown is emerald-hued,
High shelter for a nesting bird.
    It grows in Brooklyn, too.

In the Forest

It's fun to walk in the forest
In winter, spring, summer, and fall,
And search for an ovenbird's nest,
Or step on a little puffball.

It's fun to walk in the forest
And see among lofty oak trees
A scarlet tanager flying,
As if he would ignite the leaves.

It's fun to walk in the forest
And follow wild animal tracks
Without knowing the difference
Between a skunk's and a muskrat's.

Spring Morning

I look out the window
and see a robin
hunting for earthworms
on the dewy lawn.
I see a cardinal
with feathers as bright
as his half-whistled song;
two gray squirrels,
a white cat pouring herself
through a picket fence,
and a yellow butterfly –
all existing in themselves
among flowers and trees
under a blue morning sky.
My soul goes out
to meet what I see.
The spring morning swells
like a choir inside me.

Monarch Butterfly

The hungry, striped caterpillar
Munching on a milkweed leaf
Is a creature of regal disguise.
It can change itself into something else
Before your unbelieving eyes.

Before your unbelieving eyes
The caterpillar mummifies
And sleeps unseen, suspended in time.
What flower is this that flies,
Then migrates in fall to a tropic clime?

Alligator Tracks

We dock at Ship Island, a hurricane-split sandbar
boasting a Civil War fort; walk barefoot along a beach
backed by creeping, wind-ribbed dunes.
The midmorning sun gleams on the Gulf.
Gulls wheel and cry above the waves.

With a stick I overturn
the cast-off shell of a horseshoe crab –
a living fossil whose tail is so sharp-pointed
Indians once used it to arm the tips
of their fish spears.

Waist-deep we wade in the limpid water.
A black-winged shadow hugs the bottom.
Suddenly it slides away. A *stingray*.

Near the island's eastern point
we cross a tidal flat to the inner beach.
Sand-colored sandpipers run before us.
They appear, disappear
like watery ripples that spill
their lustrous lining on the beach
and then subside.

Something flushes four red-winged blackbirds
from the marshgrass. At the edge
of a shallow pool we discover
a strange trail in the sand.

A four-footed creature with sprawling gait
passed this way when the tide was out.
The length of its stride is greater than mine.
We puzzle over the splay footprints,
the unbroken line between them.
There is an absence of clawmarks,
as though the feet swung sideways into the sand,
dragging the toes as they landed.

In my mind's eye, I see
the longest backboned, cold-blooded, egg-laying flesh-eater
in North America: *Alligator mississippiensis*.
The tracks of this last living link with the dinosaur
stretch a short distance and vanish.

"Is that a log floating in the lagoon?"
"Are those knotholes or eyes?"
"In Louisiana, I saw one drag a dog underwater an' drown it."
"A log?"
"No, a ten-foot gator."

Our thoughts creep, slither, swim in the night swamp.
Our goosebumps harden into scales.
Unmoving we listen,
breathless we stare at eyes staring at us
with a red, unblinking gleam.
Something bellows but it ain't a bullfrog;
it is the night side of nature.
At my back I hear the high twangy drawl
of some shotgun-toting backwoods cracker
telling two greenhorns from Canada:
"If'n a mudpuppy barks six times at you,
you'll die 'fore sundown."

The sun is the whole sky. In its white glare
we snap close-ups of the trackway,
then creep away, skirting the marsh
lest we stumble upon a gator-hole
with a gator basking in it.

Besides sweat we now sweat fear.
Fear trickles down to our shadows rippling
on the saltwater,
onto our last can of warm Dixie beer.
Fear conjures up the cottonmouth, the hammerhead,
this barrier island at night,
where a shadow deeper than darkness
crawls out of the darkness,
and materializes into an alligator
glistening with starlight…

We reached the boat-dock by late afternoon.
A strong wind had sprung up from the south,
with a rising tide, driving a scud of whitecaps
into shore. We cast off,
and gunned the *Lady L.* toward Gulfport.
The salt spray stung our eyes.

In the Tropics

I

In a tall dead tree at the jungle's edge
the *zopilotes* gather,
waiting for death to feed them.
I pick up a stone
and hurl it at one of the black vultures,
and miss. It does not move
but regards me as an intruder.

On a paved road that skirts the jungle
an iguana gasps, tail twitching.
Its entrails glisten like jewelry.
A truck has run over it.

Circling lower and lower, a vulture
descends. Others follow.
In the heat haze their shadows converge,
swell to a seething mass of wings.

II

The road to Punta Morena plunges seaward
through jungle. Shoulder-high ferns
float on shadowy stems.
A scaly, sunstruck rock flicks its tongue at a fly.
Scattered huts with thatched roofs
squat in the green heat of midday.
Beside the road, under a banana tree,
the sun-bleached bones of some animal
shine like a white fire.

III

On this scorpion-tailed peninsula
sleep Maya gods of sun, rain, maize...
The sunbaked landscape is haunted with ruins,
on which iguanas bask and gaze.

At my back, the jungle presses.
I climb the steep limestone stairs of a pre-Columbian temple
that overlooks the sea, and listen to the murmer
of Yucatan's coral-crusted shell.

Legend has it that anyone who stays overnight in Tulum
is destined to go mad. The ancient Maya
painted human sacrificial victims blue,
adorned them with jade and gold

before cutting out their hearts with a flint knife
and throwing the corpses into a cenote.
Here beauty once flowered in death
to propitiate the gods of sun, rain, maize...

IV
    For J.C.

Although it is cruel, you cannot but marvel
at the ingenuity
of Peruvian Indian children
who have no store-bought toys to play with.
When evening comes, they catch large bats
with insects baited on fish-hooks,
and, attached to long strings,
fly them like kites in the jungle.

V

To encounter a large land crab
scuttling along the corridor
of a seaside hotel after midnight
is a startling experience.
I can talk to a dog;
but a crab is so sensitive.
Both of us froze.
                    Suddenly
the crab sidled past me,
keeping close to the wall,
sharp pincers extended.
I followed the creature outside
to the edge of the patio,
down a moonlit path
till it disappeared under
a tree's shadow.

VI

The sun was a lion's head
blazing down on the dry savanna.
A sudden fire caught the grass;
a herd of antelope exploded.

Over the rain-forest canopy
a crowned eagle soared,
then swooped. Its talons tore
a small monkey from a treetop.

A strangler fig's aerial roots –
thick as an elephant's trunk –
formed a living coffin
around the host tree it crushed.

Sensing the body heat
of a wild pig snuffling the bushes,
a leaf-clinging leech
tensed itself like a twig.

Woody vines webbed every tree.
In the green moonlight
a river snaked seaward,
shedding the land like an old skin.

VII
From wintry skies we tourists come.
Jetplanes deposit us on the tarmac.
Dazzled by the Jamaican sun,
we blink, and grope for our luggage.

Out of step with the island's rhythm,
shadowed by the stares of Rastas,
we snap the scenery – life's a beach –
go native drinking overproof rum

and smoking ganja. *No problem, mahn.*
We haggle with patois-speaking higglers.
We measure time by a bronze suntan;
then fly home, flaunting it like a badge.

The Tugboat

Whether towing or pushing barges
or boldly rubbing shoulders
with her seagoing sisters,
the tugboat is the tomboy
of the harbor.

Suburban Gothic

Almost daily, amorphous shopping malls,
pylons, high-rises, fast-food outlets
agglomerate in the suburbs
and squeeze the sky into a corner.
Parking lots spread like lava.
On Sundays, families picnic at McDonald's,
then drive several miles to admire a tree.
Ours is an age that is ageless.
Everything is disposable.
What was once meadowland
is now a muddy subdivision.
Where a birch grove stood,
a gas station squats.
The neighborhoods have a numbing sameness,
a numbing sameness, a numbing sameness...
the look of a necropolis-to-be.
Developers have named the streets
for the beauty bulldozed to build them:
Willowbrook Place, Marsh Hawk Crescent, Green Valley
     Lane...
In the wilderness of suburbia,
a person could get lost for life
and not even know it.

Zug Island

Detroit, Michigan

There is one word
and one word only
that best describes
Zug Island: *zugly*.

Toronto Is the Indian Word for Day Job

For Geordie McDonald

In the *Globe and Mail,* Canadian banks boast
of millon-dollar profits.
Today I went to the Metropolitan Toronto Reference Library.
It was closed because of budget cuts.

During our wait over dinner at the Idler Pub
My friend, an investment banker turned artist, said:
"All values are only relative to a given culture."
She ate her roast beef rare.

Geordie belongs to a musicians' union.
This dying year coughs up dismal weather.
Keeping one's dreams alive in Hogtown is a full-time
        occupation.
He surives, drumming to a different marcher.

Obit

When my dear poet friend Don Polson
(he could make a monument of a moment –
"the amber breath of apples
rising from this orchard grass..."
but was too shy to sing in public)
washed down a handful of barbiturates
with a quart of vodka
on New Year's Eve, 1989,
he knew that he would never write
a poem about it.

The Visitant

O why do you come, my enchanted one,
To visit me only when I'm dreaming?
What solitude of yours is buried in me?
What sleep of mine creates your being?

And what happens to you when I waken,
And reality comes to consciousness of time?
Do you despair of your spirit world,
Knowing that you cannot enter mine?

New Orleans Sketches

For Louise McKinney

1. *Nocturne*

Softly it rains on the attic roof.
The long-stemmed leaves of a cottonwood rustle.
Moths flutter at the window screen.
The snake-hipped black woman rubbing her body with
    coconut oil
Gets up from the sofa to draw the bamboo blind.
There are moments when the flesh
Surprises my spirit into poetry,
And nights when I inhabit a dark space
Made warm by the weight of my breathing.

2. *Sadie*

Day after day, I watch Sadie –
sweet and black as molasses –
sweating over a hot press
in a New Orleans laundry.

Sadie's long and tall. Her legs
make most women envious.
Her velvet eyes glow blacker
than her cornrow-braided hair.

At lunchtime, Sadie sits
under a big magnolia tree,
eating, chatting, laughing
with the other laundresses.

I'd ask Sadie for a date;
but I'm afraid, so afraid
the sterile whiteness of my skin
might blind her.

3. *Talk to Me Like the Rain*

In a brass bed by a French window
I waken with my hand asleep on your breast,
your leg over mine.
I kiss the back of your neck,
and you shiver with pleasure –
beautiful buttocks pressing against me.
Listen. How softly it rains
on the roofs of the Quarter.
Your sweet wetness sticks to my tongue.
Talk to me… talk to me like the rain
and let me listen
as I enter you forever.

4. *Voodoo Love*

All night long
I've been burning candle-sperm,

knowing that she lies
in another's arms,

my mind getting fucked
over and over.

5. *Terpsichore in a G-String*

When Smokin' Joe saw that leggy stripper
doing the "Night Train" bump and grind
in a Bourbon Street strip joint,
he grabbed her by the ankles
and made a wish.
How effortlessly she did the splits.

A thing of beauty was her body,
it seemed a toy forever —
pasties, sequins, G-string...
Smokin' Joe could not but ruminate:
"If life's the biggest burlesk,
love is a slow-motion rape."

6. *Jazz Requiem*

His sound I remember well.
The last time I saw him
he was cooling his habit
in some private hell.

Playin' jazz is how I pray, man.
It's my way of callin' God up
long-distance
on a pawnshop saxophone.

Hooked on the blues
he blew soul... sweated soul
to the bone.
He could really chase a chorus.

Whenever I hear a tenor sax taking the breaks,
I see eyes that look bruised
and a gold-toothed grin.
Don't dig me, man, I'm gone.

7. *In a New Orleans Cemetery*

In a New Orleans cemetery
the tombs are crowded together,
whitewashed, sculptured,
spidered with cracks,
magnolia-shaded, guarded by angels,
and epitaphed;
marbled, moss-grown, with crosses crowned,
and, strangest of all,
above ground.

My Mother Loved to Dance the Tango

My mother loved to dance the tango –
Leroy Anderson's haunting "Blue Tango."
She loved to tango with my godfather –
A tall, moustached Sicilian barber.

Step by rhythmic step – through walks, turns,
Cortes – in four-four time they moved as one.
Their bodies glided, they were the music.
Oh, how the wallflowers envied them!

My father never danced. He drank and smoked
And played *briscola* with his friends;
Stole beetle-browed glances at my mother,
Who did not want the dance to end.

Climacteric

For Clifton Whiten

The fog swallows the hard-edge cityscape.
A slug crawls over the slime its skin secretes.
Toadstools nudge through the leaf mold of autumn.
Adrift, I walk the blank streets,
My life half-mossed with middle age.
An ex-wife's allegation long ago –
You will never be happy – haunts me still.
My symptoms remind me that I exist.
My symptoms remind me that I exist.
In the harbor, a foghorn echoes itself.
I follow the granite seawall that rims the park.
The ebbed beach reeks of salt and rotting kelp.
My only beacon is a seagull.
Grant me, O Lord, the forbearance of Job.
No man is wise from another man's woe.

Words

The Bible, the Torah, the Koran –
The vain anthropocentrism of man.
Do we need myths? Should these bones live?
The computer runs algorithms
But the psyche's still primitive.

La Puttana Maria

She gazed at the silver crucifix
hanging on the wall above her bed
and remembered her first Communion
in a Calabrian hilltown church.

Now the intinction was different.
Men partook of her 17-year-old body
as though it were a sacrament.
Her white bed was the altar.

The Eternal City had buried her innocence
in a bordello.
Figlio di puttana! she cried,
flinging a satin cushion at the cross.

In Memory of Joseph Côté
(1931-1994)

Smokin' Joe – the conscience of the westend
Is laid to rest.
Joseph Côté, 63, my longtime friend…
I mourn his death.

I remember our pilgrimage to Faulkner's Rowan Oak.
We emptied a pint of bourbon
("Enough to work up a thirst," said Joe)
Onto the Great Writer's gravestone.

Joe taught language arts to highschool dropouts.
An old snapshot shows him at home, wineglass in hand,
Consulting his battered dictionary for the spelling
Of a word he said I mispronounced.

Joe's one-upmanship had panache.
Drunk one night he declaimed most of "Prufrock" by heart.
That picture I lost.
As my friend he outlasted my wives. I miss him a lot.

It's early morning, it's spring, I'm driving, Joe's smoking.
What's nirvana but a cup of coffee
In some rural Mississippi town
Where a bad day's fishing is better'n a good day's working.

"...Joseph's was a star-crossed life,"
I quote his sister, from her letter
Mailed in an envelope
Addressed to me in Joe's own handwriting.

Smokin' Joe was so *un*straight,
He rolled snake eyes with loaded dice;
Once visited me in New Orleans on Ash Wednesday.
If you're not living on the edge, you're taking up too much
    space.

He died in April –
My dear ironic friend, the conscience of the westend.
I telegraphed roses to his funeral,
A card which said: *Joe, you're only on the road again.*

My Room at the Royal Hotel

In my room at the Royal Hotel,
All time is eternally present.
Everywhere I find myself seems nothing
But a resting place between places
That become resting places
Between resting places themselves.

In my room at the Royal Hotel,
A color print of a bristlecone pine
Hangs on the wall above my bed.
The tree clings to a barren mountain ridge
And looks half plant, half mineral –
Like a tree that would grow on the moon.

In my room at the Royal Hotel,
Over my failed marriages I brood.
At twenty-three I fathered a daughter.
At fifty-three I begin to wonder
Whether the waning of the libido
Weakens the mind or lends it wings.

In my room at the Royal Hotel,
I think of Strindberg studying the occult
In his room at the Hotel Orfila.
The room reeks of hashish and sulphur.
I hear a cricket singing inside my pillow.
My insomnia would make a succubus chaste.

In my room at the Royal Hotel,
The telephone's black skull rings through its teeth.
"*Nonno* is dead," says my son's voice,
Three time zones away. I see my father
Going for his last walk in the woods.
The trees enshroud him with their shade.

In my room at the Royal Hotel,
My home away from wherever home is,
All time is eternally present.
In Vancouver, the rain rains on itself.
I go to the window. My tired eyes follow
A flock of pigeons flying nowhere.

September-October 1994

Watching My Wife Make Passatelli

I taste my childhood in passatelli –
a soup so flavorsome and nourishing…
If I were on my deathbed,
a bowl of passatelli would revive me.

In the kitchen, my wife, kerchiefed and aproned,
makes the broth for passatelli
the way my mother and my nonna used to make it.
Enraptured I watch her.

The aroma wafts me back to the house
I grew up in, in Windsor, Ontario.
Just when I start winning at marbles,
my mother's voice calls me to supper.

While the rich broth simmers,
she makes the passatelli, Romagna style.
The basis is always bread crumbs, eggs, and Parmigiano.
A little nutmeg flavors the mixture.

Each move of hers is measured.
Taking no heed of time nor of its loss,
I take aim with a glittering taw,
and send Carlo's aggie spinning into the weeds.

Proust conquered time by dipping a madeleine
into a cup of tea. The passatelli
congeal into tender strands that float
in the steaming hot broth. I taste… I see …

March 1998

Index of Titles

The *Collected Poems* of Len Gasparini keeps our attention focussed on what is, has been and will be transparent. He ranks with the few contemporary poets who understand the past as well as the present and have much to contribute to those who may still be liberate in the future. His imagination is a dark wood with wildlife in it.

Born in Windsor, Ontario, and educated at the school of hard knocks, Len Gasparini is the author of two short-story collections: *Blind Spot* and *A Demon in My View;* two children's books; a non-fiction work, *Erase me,* in a collboration with photographer Leslie Thompson; and a one-act play. He has contributed articles and book reviews to numerous journals.